A Year in the
Country

Front Cover Tim Fitzharris
Title Page Horse on a farm, Alexey Stiop/
Shutterstock

Image Credits
p. 4 Greg Latza; p. 12 FrankvandenBergh/Getty
Images; p. 34 Joshua Roberts; p. 36 Ne-Dah-Ness
Greene; p. 37 courtesy of John Boyd Jr.;
p. 38-39 Adrian Boyd/National Black Farmers
Association (2); p. 40-42 courtesy of The
Abundant Table; p. 54-59 Photos by Matthew
Breiter Photography; p. 60-62 Louis Gilbert
Photography; p. 63 courtesy of Sharon Braxton;
p. 76 David Stoeklein; p. 82 The Picture Pantry/
offset.com; p. 84: Alohaflaminggo/Shutterstock;
p. 85 Threshermen: Granada Historical Museum;
p. 86 Heebphoto/Alamy Stock Photo; p. 87 (2),
89 (3): Michael Kotutwa Johnson; p. 88: Maria
Elena Peterson; p. 90 Linda Kastiel Kozlowski; p.
91 Jewell Johnson for Dean Johnson; p. 106-109
Photos by Tim Toms Photography;
p. 115 Steer and boy: Melissa Jordan;
p. 121 Wonder Girl: Shameka Seabrook;
p. 133 Alpacas: Leanne Van Overbeke;
p. 144-145 JamesBrey/Getty Images;
p. 146-153 Photos by Richard Murphy;
p. 157 Steven Salerno; p. 161 The Long Haul: Adonia
Henry; p. 163 Joshua Zanoni; p. 178 Jason Ray
Photography/Getty Images; p. 179 Brenda Kelly/
Country magazine contributor; p. 180 Barn: Joseph
Kayne Photography

A Country Book

© 2022 RDA Enthusiast Brands, LLC.
1610 N. 2nd St., Suite 102
Milwaukee, WI 53212-3906

ISBN
978-1-62145-812-8 (dated),
978-1-62145-813-5 (undated)

Component Number
116800104H (dated),
116800106H (undated)

Text, photography and illustrations for *A Year
in the Country* are based on articles previously
published in *Country, Country Woman, Farm &
Ranch Living*, and *Birds & Blooms* magazines.

Table of Contents

WELCOME...

Ingenuity. Neighborliness. Thriftiness. Hard work. Gratitude for nature's bounty. Love of the great outdoors. Appreciation of life's simple pleasures.

These all-American values shine through in the photographs and stories collected in this beautiful celebration of the country spirit. From chronicles of day-to-day life on the farm to snapshots of soaring vistas and intimate encounters with wildlife, along with favorite recipes, clever crafts and treasured memories, *A Year in the Country* gathers the best contributions from readers of *Country, Farm & Ranch Living, Country Woman* and *Birds & Blooms* magazines this past year.

Whether you live in the country or just love the idea of being in harmony with nature, we invite you to enjoy the peace and beauty of country living all year long.

THE EDITORS

Spring

Long pricklyhead poppies boast brilliant colors in this lush field near Christine, Texas.
PHOTO BY TIM FITZHARRIS

The Good Life

LIFE IN THE COUNTRY

Each season brings something new to this corner of North Carolina.

TRUDY HAYWOOD SAUNDERS MOUNT GILEAD, NORTH CAROLINA

Clockwise from left: Town Creek Indian Mount State Historic Site is a few miles from the family home; Trudy's father, Truett; Jeff and Peyton with the catch of the day.

At a time when the world is connected by the click of a button, it is easy to think that time has forgotten our little piece of the country. Chip, North Carolina, which is nestled between the two small towns of Mount Gilead and Troy in almost the center of the state, has been forgotten in many ways. But I'm certainly not going to complain about that.

To appreciate the view from our place, which is near the Uwharrie National Forest, it's important to understand the past. In my case, our family has lived in Chip, our little community without so much as a name sign, as far back as anyone around can remember.

In fact, we believe that our family goes back 200 years here. My great-grandfather and his father before him ran the country store that bore our family name.

When I was a child, a dirt road ran in front of my house. That road has now been paved, yet many other things still remain the same.

I remember waiting impatiently for the mailman—my best friend's daddy—to stop each day as I hoped for something interesting to be put in the box. Often the mailman is still the only person who ends up driving by the residents, but these days my childhood mailman's son is the one delivering our packages.

As a child, I thought that everyone lived like this, surrounded by family and love. It wasn't until I started school that I learned many children didn't regularly see their

> *Blueberry picking still fills the sweltering July days, but we always find time to rest on the porch."*

Clockwise from left: Truett, Barbara, Trudy, Jeff and Peyton; Woods surround the family home; Peyton gives Cooter a hug.

grandparents, aunts, uncles and cousins. *How strange,* I thought.

Today, I take great pleasure in getting to share many of the same lovely aspects of country life that my ancestors enjoyed with Peyton, my 8-year-old daughter. I find a special comfort in that. Holding my daughter's hand, walking with my parents, Truett and Barbara Haywood, and friendly Cooter, the neighbors' dog who thinks he belongs to all of us, I am reminded of what is really important.

Each season brings us something brand new, while still repeating the endless cycle of life in the country. Spring ushers in the rebirth of the heirloom flowers that my grandmother grew—wonderful morning glories, four-o'clocks and the wild Queen Anne's lace that we dye with food coloring. We marvel at all of the sweet animal babies—fawns, birds that hatch in our flowerpots, turkeys, foxes and rabbits. And just about everyone counts the "buns" playing in the yard.

Summer brings a seemingly nonstop flow of garden-fresh vegetables, just like the ones my grandfather used to plant with the rusty tractor. Blueberry picking fills the sweltering July days as we load our buckets, but we find time to rest on the porch before an afternoon thunderstorm.

Soon crisp fall is ushered in, causing the oak, maple and sweet gum leaves to blush with its whispers. The season brings the family holiday meals to enjoy together.

Finally, the quiet of winter arrives, with an occasional dusting of snow—to the children's delight—and restful walks in the woods to the river with my daddy, completing a year in the life of our place in the country.

Someone once told me it was sad that I had lived in the same place all of my life, but I believe the opposite is true. What is really sad is if someone never finds a place—like ours—to truly call home.

The comforting charm of a farmhouse is timeless.

OUR FARMHOUSE STYLE

Chickens in the sink, pies cooling in the window and sweaty overalls made our home the best in the country.

WILMA VERNICH GREENBRIER, TENNESSEE

Recently I read an informal survey indicating that the "farmhouse style" of building and decorating a home is here to stay.

I find this thought very appealing. After all, I spent the first 18 years of my life growing up in a farmhouse that my dad, uncle and grandpa built. And let me tell ya—no farmhouse trending out there in a glamorous magazine matches the real living and loving that went on in my home, even if it was only 1,200 square feet.

My parents' grain farm included acres of soybean, corn and wheat fields. It also had three barns, pastures, woods, a pond and our farmhouse. Dad had said that when he finished laying the subfloor of his new farmhouse, it looked bigger than a roller skating rink.

The days started early in our sunny kitchen, where the window over the sink was framed by yellow and white gingham curtains my savvy mother made. The window did not look out over a backyard swimming pool, a fancy outdoor kitchen or a rose-covered pergola with oh-so-perfectly matched patio furniture and color-coordinated accessories. Mama's post at the kitchen sink afforded her the opportunity to keep careful watch over the chicken yard, the clothesline, her quite prolific vegetable garden and Daddy's barns.

Mama churned out three square meals a day for her family and for anyone else who was working on the farm at mealtime. She did it all on plain Formica counters and with one oven, too. No double oven, stainless steel refrigerator, computerized kitchen appliances or granite countertops in Mama's farmhouse kitchen. Her office was the kitchen.

Dad bought 200 baby chicks from the local farm co-op in spring. We kept 50 as laying hens, and we ate the rest. Over the course of the summer, I'd awaken in the morning and lumber downstairs only to see chicken feet sticking out of the kitchen sink—this was just a normal part of our morning routine.

My mother's homemade chocolate and lemon meringue pies really did cool in the open window, because we didn't have central heat and air conditioning. Dad preferred the fresh country air. He did, however, become convinced to buy a window air conditioning unit when I was about 7 years old.

Other than that window unit, fans were what cooled down our farmhouse at night. The advantage to that was the privilege of being lulled to sleep by the chirping of crickets and the aroma of the blooming honeysuckle drifting in through all the open windows.

A brick fireplace nestled in our living room made home extra cozy in the winter. Sometimes my sister and I would roast marshmallows over the crackling flames. Our fireplace did not have the ubiquitous television mounted above the mantel you'll find in homes these days.

> **No farmhouse trending out there in a glamorous magazine matches the real living and loving that went on in my childhood home.**

Some designers of farmhouse style might shudder at the sight of the various items that decorated our farmhouse. There were no trendy painted signs declaring ours a "farmhouse" or wire baskets full of fake eggs nestled in fake straw. Instead, our egg-gathering bucket was lined with an old pair of Dad's cotton underwear. The eggs inside were so fresh they might still be warm, with grass and feathers sticking to them.

After a few minutes inside our house you knew you were in a home that had seen some genuine country living. The sights and smells could really tickle your senses: muddy work boots mingled with sweaty overalls.

Fortunately, the delicious aromas outnumbered the bad ones, especially when Mama made homemade bread and cinnamon rolls. A pot of beans or sassafras roots for tea might be simmering on the stove.

The very best smell, though, wafted up from the pyramid of homemade doughnuts piled high on a platter that often greeted me when I got off the school bus in the afternoon. What a treat!

There are advantages, I suppose, to modern farmhouse design—technology that regulates thermostats and security systems by remote, gadgets that turn on the lights before you arrive home and brew a cup of coffee before your feet even hit the floor in the morning.

I wasn't born in a barn, but my son was recently married in one, and it was very nice, indeed. I imagine my father would have harrumphed loudly and muttered, "No barn like I ever had!"

I understand. Something about fetching for themselves satisfies a farm family's soul—I think it's called self-sufficiency, or is it resourcefulness? At any rate, I think it's just something inherent to our breed. Perhaps it is that indefinable essence of a decades-old, lived-in real farmhouse that makes city dwellers want to copy and live in one.

The other day I drove by a brand-new farmhouse-style home that was being built in our neighborhood. I found myself wondering about the family who would soon take up residence there. Would they have chicken feet sticking out of their kitchen sink, too?

GENERATIONS OF JOY

A visit to Great-Grandma's farm sent my children's imaginations soaring.

JACKIE HARTMAN ST. PAUL, MINNESOTA

My grandmother was 92 when my husband, Ken, and I made our final visit to the farm. As we drove down the country road, the humid, hog-scented air resurfaced deep-seated memories of making biscuits with my grandma. My sisters, cousins and I had spent much of our time outside, exploring the fields, catching lightning bugs and picking fruit from the orchards.

Those early experiences shaped who I am today, teaching me the importance of land stewardship and commitment to family. We wanted to share that joy and freedom with our kids, Eli and Norah, and for them to be able to spend time with their great-grandmother.

Amanda Hartman lived on Ricker Road for more than 60 years. In many ways she was a pioneer, and on that last visit she was as strong-willed as ever. She and my grandfather, Herbert, raised chickens without growth hormones and antibiotics. They focused on living a simple, healthy lifestyle and encouraged their children and grandchildren to do the same. When we'd visit the farm as children, we were shocked at her dietary recommendations. Avoid sugar? Reduce salt intake? Eat organic? Take vitamins? Never! Now that we are older, we fully appreciate how forward-thinking Amanda was. "If only we had listened more," we lament. She was the family matriarch, and she built a legacy that has had a lasting impact on her descendants.

Upon arrival, Ken, the kids and I ran up the steps and opened the screen door. Grandma was waiting for us, sitting at the kitchen table with a huge smile and open arms. By this time, she was homebound. Although healthy eating was a big part of her life, decades of hard work had taken their toll. Her mobility was limited, and this was difficult to see and accept. We'd grown accustomed to finding her in the utility room canning fruit or preserving vegetables, but this visit was different. Instead of joining us as we explored the wonders of the farm landscape, Grandma watched us experience her beloved farm from a distance.

Eli and Norah were eager to check things out, so off we went. Our first stop was to make an obstacle course of tractor tires. We found the tires in the old barn. They were thick with dust and dirt, but no amount of filth was going to keep us from enjoying them. We arranged them into a series of contests and took turns rolling them over finish lines. The kids were thrilled to have the freedom to create as many games as their imaginations would allow. There were very few restrictions or parent-imposed rules. Grandma watched the fun from the family room, relishing her great-grandchildren's laughter.

As we played, we saw a cat repeatedly return to a spot on the lawn. Curious, we ran over to find that it was attempting to unearth a rabbit's nest, where three baby bunnies were taking shelter from the day's sunlight. The kids were excited to see these tiny, helpless creatures, but they were also worried. Hope for their survival seemed limited out there in the open.

We brainstormed our options. Would we let nature determine their outcome? We carefully pulled their little bodies out of the fur-lined nest and ran inside to

Top to bottom: the happy couple in their garden around 1968; Amanda and Herbert on their wedding day in 1940; Amanda as a child.

Amanda's entire family gathered at the farm to celebrate her birthday in 2004. Jackie and Ken (in a blue shirt, with a hand on Jackie's dad's shoulder) are on the right.

show Grandma. Then she listened to our concern and shared some wisdom. After decades on the farm, she knew all about life and death. We decided to relocate the little rabbits to a more secure location, hoping their mother would find them before the cat did.

Behind the farm were a few acres of woodland. As kids, my siblings and I had spent hours in those woods, exploring and fearfully imagining what was lurking within. The familiar smell of corn and dirt accompanied us as we trekked toward the woods on the same path that I had taken so often as a child. Slapping at mosquitoes, we charged into the buzzing wilderness,

> **Slapping at mosquitoes, we charged into the buzzing wilderness, searching for trees to climb."**

searching for trees to climb. Before long Norah was 10 feet off the ground, her brother pushing ahead into the tangled forest. We emerged from those woods with scratches, bug bites and plenty of stories to share with Grandma.

"Great-Grandma! Guess what we've been doing!" the kids exclaimed. My grandma's eyes widened as the kids described their adventures. She inspected their bumps and bruises and laughed at their vivid portrayals. Their excitement spilled over into the kitchen as we got our meal ready.

After we ate, Eli and Norah ran back outside to play, the screen door slamming behind them. I could see them through the window, their imaginations at work. "Grandma, come see this," I said as I finished the dishes.

Tears welled in my grandmother's eyes as we watched her great-grandkids climb onto a large rock. They were experiencing life as she had always seen it, as it always had been on the farm—a world of simple, remarkable beauty.

IN TROUBLING TIMES

Who needs television when there's a family of hummingbirds in the backyard?

MARION BALL TUCSON, ARIZONA

Costa's hummingbirds reside year-round in Arizona, so my feeder is always full. The birds that visit the yard have grown used to us and tolerate our inquisitive nature.

When mid-February 2020 came, a female Costa's hummingbird built a nest on our Mexican fence post cactus. She finished her nest by Feb. 19, and she laid her first egg on Feb. 22. Two days later, she laid a second egg.

To my surprise, 18 days after she laid the first egg, both eggs hatched! I was used to eggs hatching in the order they were laid, from my observations of bluebird, tree swallow and chickadee nest boxes.

The joy of baby hummingbirds was quickly overshadowed by the spread of COVID-19 in the United States and three weeks of fickle weather: sunny and warm, storms followed by cold spells, overcast skies, rain and 30-plus mph winds.

The hatchlings were just 8 days old when we had a full day of rain and cold temperatures. When I noticed Mom had left to hunt for food, I put an umbrella over the cactus so the nest and the young birds would stay dry. When Mom returned, she flew under the umbrella and into the nest. Though it was a cold and miserable day, the little family stayed dry.

I spent a lot of time outside watching the mother feeding and taking care of her young. She was such a good mom, making sure each hatchling had enough to eat.

Days before the hatchlings fledged, Mom became more elusive and aggressive. She did not allow other hummingbirds into the yard. Other hummingbirds, of course, managed to sneak into the yard when she was out looking for food.

The youngsters fledged on the morning of April 1. The stronger baby left the nest first and flew to the 6-foot wall. Not to be outdone, the second baby flew from the nest into the lime tree. I was very lucky to capture a family portrait.

Over the years, it has been a great joy of mine to watch birds. I'm so very grateful to them for reminding me that life in all its forms is precious. Seeing these sweet hummingbirds take flight on their life journeys helped me to overcome my worries about the global pandemic.

Left: Marion took comfort from watching this hummingbird family. Right: eggs in a nest.

Scrapbook

CAPTURE THE BEAUTY AROUND YOU

2

1. SCENIC BEAUTY

Fireweed blooms brightly on the Alaska Peninsula near Popof Island.

CALLEN DAVIS PORT ALSWORTH, ALASKA

2. WELCOME VISITORS

Cedar waxwings visited me for the first time two years ago in May. They love my old mulberry tree! I hoped they would come back the next year, and I was thrilled to see more than 50 of them.

ANITA STEVENS FAIRMONT, WEST VIRGINIA

1. BEACON OF SAFETY
Fisgard Lighthouse in British Columbia is the oldest lighthouse on Canada's west coast.

ANN MARIE EBERHART
GIG HARBOR, WASHINGTON

2. PICK YOUR PLEASURE
Dahlia farms add to the scenic beauty along the picturesque drive to Mount Hood in Oregon.

JIMMIE McCARTY
STARKVILLE, MISSISSIPPI

3. ROOM TO RUN
This photo captures the pure bliss that my dog Penny and I feel when we can spend some time under the sun in New Mexico's Sangre de Cristo Mountains.

ALYSSA ELLEGAARD
FERTILE, MINNESOTA

1. BETTER THAN CAKE

I celebrated my 30th birthday by hiking a trail in Lake McMurtry Park with my husband, Joel, and our dog, Loki.

EMILY BILLINGS STILLWATER, OKLAHOMA

2. WARM FUZZIES

My daughter, Lindsay, hatched these baby Sebastopol geese just a few days before this picture was taken.

BRENDA LOUTHIAN BOONES MILL, VIRGINIA

3. FROM THE TOP

This is the view from Spruce Knob Lake in West Virginia's Monongahela National Forest. It is the highest point in West Virginia. The scenery is truly nature at its best!

SUSAN RUFENER ORRVILLE, OHIO

PAINTERLY MAGIC
The colors and texture of the water
and clouds at Edgewater Park in
Cleveland, Ohio, look just like art
on canvas.

RICK DEAL STRONGSVILLE, OHIO

1. TOWERING TREES

I'm so thankful for the time we had together as a family in Washington's Quinault Rain Forest. In this lush temperate forest, you realize just how small you are.

VALERIE BOWLS RICHLAND, WASHINGTON

2. TRAIL BUDDY

On a foggy morning hike in Virginia's Grayson Highlands State Park, my friend Nathaniel and I encountered a wild pony enjoying a snack along Wilburn Ridge.

BO STEWART BOLIVAR, PENNSYLVANIA

3. A PEACEFUL PLACE

Spring! Ah, a breath of fresh air here in Maryland. Color comes to life along with trees and flowers. This is a time that I love working busily in my little flower house. This tiny space brings such joy to all who visit.

DANITA BLY
WESTMINSTER, MARYLAND

1. EVERLASTING BEAUTY
I have hiked the Waterrock Knob Trail (at milepost 451.2 on the Blue Ridge Parkway) many times, and the views never get old.

MYRON CARTER
MAGGIE VALLEY, NORTH CAROLINA

2. BABY DOLLS
This is my son Brantley, enjoying the sunset with a calf that was born just that morning.

JORDAN MORTON
McCONNELLSBURG, PENNSYLVANIA

3. IN FULL COLOR
As spring migration occurs, crabapples and other flowering trees are in full bloom in my area. I had the pleasure of photographing this male Baltimore oriole among the flowers.

SCOTT DIEDRICH
BUFFALO, NEW YORK

1. PERFECT GATHERING PLACE

My parents' home in Union City, Missouri, is quintessential country, with two barns, a garden and trees. The family gathers here for homemade food, fishing, four-wheeler rides and playing on the swing set. The pond is definitely one of the highlights of my parents' property.

AMY WILER O'FALLON, MISSOURI

2. PETAL PUSHER

This wooden wagon was made in Pigeon Forge, Tennessee. I hand-painted it and call it "Billie's Painted Wagon Debut at Easter Time."

BILLIE FARRER CHATTANOOGA, TENNESSEE

3. HELLO, FRIEND

Our 6-year-old son spoils Sam the ram with some feed and a good scratchin'.

TRISHA MURDOCK POCAHONTAS, ARKANSAS

3

1. WHIRLWIND JOURNEY
I loved Montana's Glacier National Park, a stop on my 32-day road trip to 13 national parks on my summer break from teaching!

AUSTIN HOWARD SMYRNA, GEORGIA

2. SMOOTH AS GLASS
This pretty Atlantic puffin in Maine's Acadia National Park was as calm as the water around it.

RYAN BAER FREELAND, MARYLAND

3. AT HOME IN THE FIELDS
Grow where you're planted, I thought, upon seeing this day-old calf tucked under the tomatoes in my garden.

BETH MORRISON SALINA, KANSAS

Heart & Soul

FEEL THE LOVE OF COUNTRY

FARMER JOHN

Meet John Boyd Jr., an agriculture activist and the founder of the National Black Farmers Association.

CHANDRA THOMAS WHITFIELD

Stop by John Boyd Jr.'s 1,300-acre farm in Mecklenburg County, Virginia, on any given day—especially in the early morning hours—and you're bound to catch him perched atop his Case International 7150 tractor, looking toward the horizon as he rolls up and down the rows of his meticulously planted soybean, wheat and corn crops.

With each pass through the rows, John, a fourth-generation farmer, delves deeper into a sense of solitude and serenity—what he calls "being at one with nature and with God." Those who know him well say that this is where he thinks best; it's his happy place, a source of peace and his own little slice of heaven on earth. These moments of quiet contemplation in the crisp morning air, amid a chorus of chirping birds, best embody his pure love for working the land.

"There's no telling what's going through his mind when he's on that tractor," says Tony Whittingham, who has called John a friend and confidant since they met in ninth grade in the halls of Park View High School in South Hill, Virginia. "He's one of the smartest people I know—he really thinks on a different level. The best way for me to describe him is that there's an edge to his thinking. He's different and he has a heart for people and a sincere love for family."

That side of John, his colleagues and his friends agree, often ends up eclipsed by his public persona as a businessman,

Born in New York, John Boyd Jr. and his brother moved south with their parents to the family farm when John was 13 years old. He has been a farmer ever since, and he is a tireless advocate for marginalized farmers.

outspoken civil rights activist and the founder and president of the National Black Farmers Association.

His role with the NBFA frequently lands him in the national spotlight.

A FARMER'S LEGACY

John, 56, was born in Brooklyn, New York, but he came to embrace the slower pace of rural life—albeit reluctantly at first—after his parents moved the family to Virginia. John was 13, a middle school student. "If you don't want to work hard, don't be a farmer," he says. "But if you want gratification from your work— you know, from seeing that crop grow to seeing it harvested and going to the combines—it's the most rewarding occupation that you could do as far as clean, healthy work."

Known for his husky voice, hearty laugh and an affinity for cowboy hats (the bigger the better), John founded the NBFA in 1995. Today the organization, which still advocates for equality in farming, boasts a robust membership across 42 states. John says he has committed his life to fighting for Black farmers everywhere.

Like his father, grandfather and great-grandfather before him, John is a farmer through and through. In fact, his great-grandfather, who came to America in shackles as an enslaved man, eventually managed to purchase his own land—no small accomplishment in the post-Civil War era in the South. Family legend has it that each night he slept with the deed to his farm underneath his pillow.

John spent nearly 15 years as a chicken farmer and also managed tobacco crops before settling on the beans, grains and cattle that he and his wife, Kara, who shares his deep love for the land, raise on their farm in Baskerville, Virginia.

"Ever since we were kids, that's all he's ever done," says Tony. "In ninth grade and all through high school—you know, Future Farmers of America and work on the farm. Multiple generations of his family have been involved with farming. At the end of the day, that's all he knows."

It's backbreaking work. But, John insists, it's also the most fulfilling—so much so that he has tried for years to convince his adult sons, both in their 20s, to commit to taking it over one day.

"To pass along that family legacy would be a lifelong dream," he says. Thus far it has been a losing battle. They, like many in the younger generation, aren't sold on the profession. That heartbreaking reality, John says, fuels his long-standing crusade to attract young people to the field; it's an effort he says he'll maintain until he takes his last breath.

Los Angeles-based film and television producer Jeff Brick worked closely with John during the filming of *The American Farm*, a 2019 History Channel docuseries that featured the Boyd family. Jeff says he has no doubt that John will persevere.

"John Boyd is a force of nature. There is never a problem that is too difficult for him to take on and ultimately overcome,"

John grows wheat, corn, soybeans and timber and raises beef cattle on his 1,300-acre farm in Mecklenburg County, Virginia.

Proud farm family: John stands with his mother, Betty Jean; daughter, Sydni Faith; son John Wesley Boyd III; and father, John Boyd Sr.

says Jeff. "He has dealt with constant adversity in his life and career since the beginning, but wakes up every morning unfazed and ready to attack a new day. He's an indefatigable advocate for Black farmers in the United States, a hard worker, shrewd, smart and a devoted family man."

If John's unconventional credentials are any indication, Jeff is right.

MAN ON A MISSION

John Boyd Jr. is not your average farmer. Not many people, let alone farmers, can say they've met with numerous United States presidents, vice presidents and representatives. John has also had the opportunity to testify before the House Committee on Agriculture and was once vetted as a contender for the role of U.S. Secretary of Agriculture. It's all part of what he considers his calling in life: a pointed and purposeful mission to fight for equality and justice on behalf of Black farmers who, as a group, have long been marginalized and pushed out of the industry due to racial discrimination. John says that this is the central reason he founded the NBFA and why, more than 25 years later, he remains hands on and the primary face of the organization.

"I have to help educate, especially Black people in this country. Land ownership and the ability to produce your food are two of the most powerful tools that you can possess—second only to devoting your life to Jesus Christ," says John. "The ability to own land and grow your own food is a very, very powerful tool."

He continues: "My grandfather used to say, 'If you don't have any land, you don't have any power. If you don't have any food, you're bound to starve yourself to death.' And this was a man with a third-grade education."

John has been particularly vocal about federal loan discrimination—the fact that, for generations, Black farmers have been shut out of the USDA's intricate system of subsidies and federal farming programs that can be the lifeblood of successful farming operations. And he says he has experienced it firsthand, starting in the 1980s when he was repeatedly denied USDA loans for which he met the criteria. That experience opened his eyes to a backlog of unresolved discrimination cases filed against the agency.

The issue is so extremely close to his heart that he once hitched up two mules, aptly named 40 Acres and Justice, and drove his wagon 280 miles from Virginia to Washington, D.C., to draw attention to it.

With the support of the NBFA, a class-action racial discrimination case filed against the USDA on behalf of Black farmers resulted in a $1.15 billion settlement that Roll Call deemed "the biggest congressional victory in history for Black farmers." John also helped drum up support for a follow-up: the passage of a federal law in 2010 that ensured that all settlements would be awarded to eligible recipients.

BY THE NUMBERS

John says he's deeply concerned about the shrinking number of Black farmers in the United States. "Our numbers have dwindled from the turn of the century," says John, noting that there were nearly a million nonwhite farm operators in this

country at that time. And the USDA's 1910 Census of Agriculture shows that more than 240,000 of these farmers were owner-operators.

"When animals and species become endangered," John says, "Congress acts to preserve them and make sure that they survive. So we can save the snail darter, the bald eagle and the rockfish, but we haven't put any real laws in place to help preserve the oldest occupation in history for Black people, which is farming."

The number of farmers has decreased across the board, but the drop has been especially precipitous among African Americans. According to the 2017 ag census, there are fewer than 50,000 Black farmers in the United States—just 1.4% of the country's 3.4 million farmers—and those who remain in the industry tend to make substantially less money than their white counterparts. (The net cash income of the average Black-owned farm in the United States is $3,509, compared to $43,608 for white-owned farms.)

This income disparity is due in part to land ownership imbalances. The 2017 USDA report found that Black people own 29,788 farms in the U.S., totaling just over 2.5 million acres in farmland. By contrast, white people own nearly 2 million farms, totaling close to 501 million acres. In other words, Black people own less than 0.5% of the amount of farmland owned by white people. These numbers gain even greater significance when viewed alongside racial demographics of the U.S., where whites make up 60.1% of the total population and Blacks make up 13.4%.

THE WORK CONTINUES

John is doing his part to help. Diversity recruitment has long topped the NBFA's agenda, which also includes efforts to help

increase Black farmers' access to credit, initiatives meant to draw more resources to small farmers, and beefed-up education and entrepreneurship programming aimed at attracting more young people— especially young people of color—to work in agriculture.

Producer Jeff says John's dedication to his work, both on and off the farm, shines through in *The American Farm*. He recalls an especially moving scene from filming that he believes best captures John's significance to the agricultural industry.

"There was a moment, early in the first days of planting season, when I stood with John on a hillside of his farm, looking down into a hand-dug well that was at least 150 years old. He'd uncovered the well while tilling the soil with his John Deere tractor, which he bought in the 1980s and repaired countless times," Jeff remembers. "As he looked down into the darkness and hand-stacked stones, he

Above: John hosts the governor of Virginia and others at his farm.
Right: John leads a group of farmers rallying in D.C. in support of the Black farmers bill.

said, 'Lot of history in that well.' It struck me then that on the day this well was dug, John, as a Black man, wouldn't have been standing over it as the landowner that he is today."

In recent months during the ongoing pandemic, John says that he has been traveling less and staying closer to home. Staying put has allowed him to have some time to regroup and to spend more time with family—and particularly with his parents, John Sr. and Betty Jean, for whom John and Kara share full-time caregiving duties.

Seeing his parents, he says, inspires him to keep his hope alive that pushing for change is making a difference.

"It reminds me of a message I always share in my presentations," John says. "Give it time and don't give up. Don't give up on our country, don't give up on civil rights and don't give up on bringing our country closer together."

Abundant Table board member Erynn Smith hosts a group of students at the farm.

FARMING FOR GOOD

A woman-led nonprofit farm nurtures its community, as well
as the land and those who tend it.

JILL GLEESON

It's a brilliantly sunny day in Ventura County, on a squarish piece of land near the Southern California coast.

At The Abundant Table farm, between the cities of Camarillo and Oxnard, the temperature is in the mid-60s; fine for the cool-weather veggies growing with great enthusiasm on the farm's 4 acres. Just four people tend the rows of plants, which include everything from greens such as

kale and spinach, to cabbage, broccoli, turnips, carrots, beets, radishes and strawberries. "Anything that's a row crop and that's in season, we're probably growing it," says Reyna Ortega, who serves as The Abundant Table's interim executive director.

But what's remarkable about this farm isn't so much what's grown there; it's how it's grown—and why. The Abundant Table is a nonprofit, certified organic venture, all about "valuing land," says Erynn Smith, who is the former farm education director of The Abundant Table and a current board member. "It's about valuing connection with land, valuing care for the land and valuing connection and care for those who tend the land."

MAKING THE MISSION A REALITY

There are many ways that this mission materializes at The Abundant Table. It all begins with organic farming, which is sustained by practices including crop rotation, water conservation and cover cropping. The mission continues and develops further through how and where the essential fruits of this labor are then distributed. While the farm sells its fruits and vegetables through such traditional avenues as local markets and restaurants, its produce is also available farther afield to people lacking access to affordable and nutritious food.

Among the ways the farm reaches out to those of less financial means is by donating a portion of its harvest to area organizations that serve people experiencing food insecurity.

The farm sends fruits and veggies to local schools where at least 50% of the children qualify for federally assisted food initiatives. Along with its regular community supported agriculture (CSA) farm share program, The Abundant Table is home to a special Indigenous CSA, which was founded in order to supply fresh produce at reasonable prices to families of farmworkers throughout Ventura County.

Closer to home, the farm makes sure that its own workers are able to afford to purchase produce and other necessities for a healthy lifestyle by providing them not only with a fair wage, but also with health benefits.

Founded in 2009, the farm grew out of an Episcopal and Lutheran campus ministry at California State University Channel Islands. The goals were to minister from within Ventura County's large agricultural community and to provide useful farming internship opportunities for young adults after college. But the deeper mission, according to Reyna, "was really stewarding and caring for creation."

A NEW WAY TO FARM

The mission has continued through the farm's newest incarnation. Last May, The Abundant Table transitioned to a nonprofit worker cooperative with five members, four of whom are women.

"There is shared decision-making, and all collective members' voices are active in making decisions about how we work," Reyna, who speaks Spanish, explains through Erynn, who interprets for her. "And so the decisions about the farm are made by the folks who are working the most closely with the farm. It's hugely beneficial to have that shared decision-making. It creates space for us to be learning deeply as we go together."

The Abundant Table's farming method encourages women to take leadership roles, Reyna says. Before she arrived at the farm, Reyna was a longtime worker at massive industrial farms, where she says she found that limitations had been placed "on what women could and could not do."

"But here, we're farming in a system where there's a lot of responsibility for learning and doing," she says. "And for those who are willing and able to do that, there are not really any limits on how far they can go."

This responsibility is meant not only for members of The Abundant Table —it extends to area students through an initiative called Farm-Based Education. One of The Abundant Table's longest-running, most successful projects, the program brings youth of all ages to the farm to learn about everything from plant-based nutrition and cooking to "every kind of science standard that's in existence," says Erynn, who founded the program. "The farm is such a vibrant place to teach nutrient cycles in soil, water cycles, plant parts, biology and chemistry. Kids are experiencing those scientific concepts hands-on, and so it's just such a joyful learning experience."

ROOTED IN FAITH

Joyful is a good description for the farm, and that is no doubt significantly due to the faith that runs through it. While the Episcopal and Lutheran churches no longer have a role in the daily operation of The Abundant Table, their values and spirituality remain firmly rooted in it.

Taste of the Country

VEGETARIAN SKILLET ENCHILADAS

TAKES 25 min. **MAKES** 4 servings

- 1 Tbsp. canola oil
- 1 medium onion, chopped
- 1 medium sweet red pepper, chopped
- 2 garlic cloves, minced
- 1 can (15 oz.) black beans, rinsed and drained
- 1 can (10 oz.) enchilada sauce
- 1 cup frozen corn
- 2 tsp. chili powder
- ½ tsp. ground cumin
- ⅛ tsp. pepper
- 8 corn tortillas (6 in.), cut into ½-in. strips
- 1 cup shredded Mexican cheese blend

  Optional: Chopped fresh cilantro, sliced avocado, sliced radishes, sour cream and lime wedges

1. Preheat oven to 400°. Heat oil in 10-in. cast-iron or other ovenproof skillet over medium-high heat.

2. Add onion and pepper; cook and stir until tender, 2-3 minutes. Add garlic; cook about 1 minute longer. Stir in beans, enchilada sauce, corn, chili powder, cumin, pepper and tortilla strips.

3. Bring the mixture to a boil. Reduce heat; simmer, uncovered, 3-5 minutes or until tortillas are softened. Sprinkle with cheese. Bake, uncovered, until bubbly and cheese is melted, 3-5 minutes. If desired, garnish with listed optional ingredients.

1½ CUPS 307 cal., 14g fat (5g sat. fat), 25mg chol., 839mg sod., 33g carb. (5g sugars, 7g fiber), 14g pro.

FLAVORFUL TOMATO SOUP

TAKES 15 min. **MAKES** 2 servings

- ¼ cup finely chopped onion
- 1 Tbsp. butter
- ¼ tsp. dried basil
- ¼ tsp. paprika
- ⅛ tsp. garlic powder
- 1 can (10¾ oz.) condensed tomato soup, undiluted
- 1 cup 2% milk
- Fresh basil leaves, optional

In a saucepan, cook and stir onion in butter until tender. Add the basil, paprika and garlic powder. Stir in the soup and milk until well blended. Cook over medium heat until heated through, 6-8 minutes. Top with basil leaves if desired.

1 CUP 233 cal., 8g fat (5g sat. fat), 24mg chol., 989mg sod., 33g carb. (22g sugars, 2g fiber), 7g pro.

TOASTED CLUBS WITH DILL MAYO

TAKES 20 min. **MAKES** 2 servings

- 2 Tbsp. fat-free mayonnaise
- ¼ tsp. dill weed
- ¾ tsp. lemon juice, divided
- ⅛ tsp. pepper
- 4 slices whole wheat bread, toasted
- 4 thin slices deli roast beef
- 4 thin slices deli ham
- 2 slices reduced-fat provolone cheese
- 2 Bibb lettuce leaves
- 2 slices tomato
- 2 center-cut bacon strips, cooked and crumbled
- ¼ cup alfalfa sprouts
- ¼ medium ripe avocado, peeled and sliced

1. In a small bowl, combine the mayonnaise, dill, ¼ tsp. lemon juice and pepper; spread over toast. Layer 2 slices of toast with beef, ham, cheese, lettuce, tomato, bacon and sprouts.

2. Drizzle avocado with the remaining ½ tsp. lemon juice; then place over sprouts. Top with remaining 2 slices of toast.

1 SANDWICH 328 cal., 13g fat (4g sat. fat), 47mg chol., 1056mg sod., 29g carb. (6g sugars, 6g fiber), 26g pro.

TOAD IN THE HOLE BACON SANDWICH

TAKES 15 min. **MAKES** 2 servings

- 4 slices sourdough bread
- 2 Tbsp. mayonnaise
- 2 large eggs
- 2 slices cheddar cheese
- 4 cooked bacon strips

1. Using a biscuit cutter or round cookie cutter, cut out center of 2 slices of bread (discard centers or save for another use). Spread mayonnaise on 1 side of each bread slice. In a large skillet coated with cooking spray, lightly toast 1 cutout slice, mayonnaise side down, over medium-low heat. Flip; crack an egg into the center. Add 1 whole bread slice, mayonnaise side down, to skillet; Top with 1 slice cheddar cheese and 2 strips bacon.

2. Cook, covered, until egg white is set, yolk is soft-set and cheese has begun to melt. If needed, flip slice with the egg to finish cooking. To assemble, use solid slice as bottom and cutout slice as top. Repeat with remaining ingredients for second sandwich.

1 SANDWICH 610 cal., 34g fat (11g sat. fat), 240mg chol., 1220mg sod., 46g carb. (4g sugars, 2g fiber), 30g pro.

GORGONZOLA TOMATOES ON ENDIVE

TAKES 25 min. **MAKES** 20 stuffed leaves

- 20 leaves Belgian endive (about 2 heads)
- 2 medium tomatoes, seeded and finely chopped
- 3 green onions, thinly sliced
- ½ cup crumbled Gorgonzola cheese
- ½ cup chopped walnuts, toasted
- ⅓ cup balsamic vinaigrette

Arrange endive on a serving platter. In each endive leaf, layer tomatoes, onions, cheese and walnuts. Drizzle each with vinaigrette. Chill until serving.

1 STUFFED LEAF 49 cal., 4g fat (1g sat. fat), 3mg chol., 84mg sod., 4g carb. (1g sugars, 2g fiber), 2g pro. Diabetic exchanges: 1 fat.

ROTISSERIE CHICKEN PANINI

TAKES 20 min. **MAKES** 2 servings

- 3 Tbsp. mayonnaise
- 4½ tsp. grated Parmesan cheese
- 1 tsp. lemon juice
- ½ tsp. prepared pesto
- ¼ tsp. grated lemon zest
  Dash pepper
- 4 slices sourdough bread
- ¼ lb. sliced rotisserie chicken
- 4 slices ready-to-serve fully cooked bacon
- 2 slices smoked part-skim mozzarella cheese
- 2 slices red onion, separated into rings
- 4 slices tomato
- 2 Tbsp. butter, melted

1. In a small bowl, combine the first 6 ingredients and spread half the mixture over 2 bread slices (about 1 Tbsp. per slice).

2. Layer with chicken, bacon, mozzarella cheese, onion and tomato. Spread the remaining mayonnaise mixture on the remaining 2 bread slices; place them over top. Brush outsides of sandwiches with melted butter.

3. Cook sandwiches on a panini maker or indoor grill until bread is browned and cheese is melted, 3-4 minutes.

1 SANDWICH 653 cal., 42g fat (16g sat. fat), 80mg chol., 996mg sod., 40g carb. (3g sugars, 2g fiber), 28g pro.

1. Preheat oven to 350°. Line 16 muffin cups with paper or foil liners. Press the warm jam through a fine-mesh strainer. Discard pulp.

2. In a large bowl, cream butter and sugar until light and fluffy, 5-7 minutes. Add the egg whites, 1 at a time, beating well after each addition. Beat in strained jam and vanilla. In a small bowl, whisk milk and sour cream until smooth. In another bowl, whisk flour, baking powder, baking soda and salt; add to creamed mixture alternately with milk mixture, beating well after each addition. If desired, stir in red food coloring.

3. Fill prepared muffin cups three-fourths full. Bake until a toothpick inserted in center comes out clean, 20-25 minutes. Cool 10 minutes before removing to wire racks to cool completely.

4. For frosting, in a large bowl, beat cream until it begins to thicken. Add confectioners' sugar, jam and vanilla; beat until the mixture forms stiff peaks. Spread or pipe frosting over the cupcakes; refrigerate leftover frosting. Garnish cupcakes with strawberries if desired.

1 CUPCAKE 353 cal., 21g fat (13g sat. fat), 60mg chol., 184mg sod., 38g carb. (27g sugars, 0 fiber), pro.

STRAWBERRY CUPCAKES WITH WHIPPED CREAM FROSTING

PREP 20 min. **BAKE** 20 min. + cooling
MAKES 16 cupcakes

- ½ cup seedless strawberry jam or preserves, warmed
- ¾ cup butter, softened
- 1 cup sugar
- 3 large egg whites, room temperature
- 1 tsp. vanilla extract
- 1 cup 2% milk
- ½ cup sour cream
- 1⅔ cups all-purpose flour
- 1 tsp. baking powder
- ¼ tsp. baking soda
- ¼ tsp. salt
  Red food coloring, optional

FROSTING
- 2 cups heavy whipping cream
- ⅓ cup confectioners' sugar
- ⅓ cup seedless strawberry jam or preserves
- ½ tsp. vanilla extract
  Fresh strawberries, optional

DELI TURKEY LETTUCE WRAPS

TAKES 25 min. **MAKES** 2 servings

- 2 tsp. olive oil
- ½ medium red onion, thinly sliced
- 6 oz. sliced deli turkey, coarsely chopped
- 6 cherry tomatoes, halved
- 2 tsp. balsamic vinegar
- 6 Bibb or Boston lettuce leaves
- ½ medium ripe avocado, peeled and cubed
- ¼ cup shredded Swiss cheese
- ¼ cup alfalfa sprouts, optional

1. In a large skillet, heat oil over medium-high heat. Add onion; cook and stir until tender, 3-4 minutes. Add turkey; heat through. Stir in tomatoes and vinegar just until everything is combined.

2. Serve in lettuce leaves. Top with avocado, cheese and, if desired, sprouts.

3 LETTUCE WRAPS 270 cal., 16g fat (4g sat. fat), 43mg chol., 799mg sod., 11g carb. (4g sugars, 4g fiber), 22g pro. Diabetic exchanges: 3 lean meat, 1½ fat, 1 vegetable.

ONE-PAN CHICKEN RICE CURRY

TAKES 30 min. **MAKES** 4 servings

- 2 Tbsp. butter, divided
- 1 medium onion, halved and thinly sliced
- 2 Tbsp. all-purpose flour
- 1 Tbsp. curry powder
- ½ tsp. salt
- ½ tsp. pepper
- 1 lb. boneless skinless chicken breasts, cut into 1-in. pieces
- 1 can (14½ oz.) reduced-sodium chicken broth
- 1 cup uncooked instant rice
   Chopped fresh cilantro leaves, optional

1. In a large nonstick skillet, heat 1 Tbsp. butter over medium-high heat; cook and stir onion slices until tender and lightly browned, 3-5 minutes. Remove from pan.

2. In a bowl, mix flour and seasonings; toss with chicken.

3. In same skillet, heat the remaining 1 Tbsp. butter over medium-high heat. Add chicken; cook 4-6 minutes, occasionally turning, until no longer pink.

4. Stir in broth and onion; bring to a boil. Stir in rice. Remove from heat; let stand, covered, about 5 minutes or until rice is tender (mixture will be saucy). If desired, sprinkle with cilantro.

1 CUP 300 cal., 9g fat (4g sat. fat), 78mg chol., 658mg sod., 27g carb. (2g sugars, 2g fiber), 27g pro. Diabetic exchanges: 3 lean meat, 2 starch, 1½ fat.

Handcrafted

CREATE A FEELING OF HOME

FLOWER PILLOW

WHAT YOU'LL NEED

1 yd. fabric in linen blend, linen, denim or chambray

Coordinating thread

Adhesive printable embroidery paper

3 skeins green embroidery floss

1 skein yellow embroidery floss

13 flower-shaped buttons

12x16-in. pillow form

Embroidery needle

Scissors

Iron

DIRECTIONS

1. Cut fabric to 17x30 in.

2. Stitch a ½-in. rolled hem on both short sides of the fabric; press hems.

3. Fold fabric in half with right sides together and hemmed edges meeting. Mark the center fold at edges. Unfold fabric with right side facing up.

4. Bring the bottom hemmed edge to the center marks and pin in place at sides. Bring top hemmed edge down to 4 in. below center line, creating an envelope. Pin at sides.

5. Stitch the sides with a ½-in. seam, then turn right side out and press.

6. Enlarge template to fit an 8½x11-in. page. Copy template onto printable embroidery paper.

7. Cut out template, leaving a 1-in. margin. Peel off paper backing and adhere template to center of pillow front—bottom embroidery line will be about 4 in. from bottom of pillow front.

8. Embroider over template with green floss, using backstitches for stems and ground, and lazy daisy stitches for leaves. Remove adhesive template according to package instructions. Stitch buttons to tops of stems using yellow floss.

9. Insert pillow form.

WALL ART

WHAT YOU'LL NEED
Wood frame
Wood to fit in frame
Buttons
Hot glue gun
Stain, optional
Foam brush or rag, optional

DIRECTIONS

1. Stain wood and frame, if desired. Dry thoroughly.
2. Sketch chicken or alternate shape onto wood.
3. Arrange buttons to fill in space, varying sizes. Hot-glue buttons into place. Hot-glue eye, comb and feet details into place using contrasting buttons.
4. Insert into frame.

PAPER CLIPS

WHAT YOU'LL NEED
Buttons with flat backs and no shank
Large coated paper clips
Industrial glue

DIRECTIONS

1. Apply glue to back of buttons and clips. Press to adhere.
2. Allow to dry 24 hours.

Summer

Armchairs invite peaceful contemplation at Hume Lake near Kings Canyon National Park in central California.
PHOTO BY RON AND PATTY THOMAS

The Good Life

FAMILY AT THE FOREFRONT

Cattle, horses, crops and three home-schooled kids: Ranching is a family affair for this pair from the North Star State.

RACHEL CONNELL STAPLES, MINNESOTA

My name is Rachel Connell, and my life has revolved around agriculture since the day I was born. My family lived on a 29-acre farm, and when I was about 5, my parents (Mike and Mary Sams) moved us to a 208-acre ranch in the deep backwoods of central Minnesota. My brother, Matthew, and I ran through the woods, waded in the creek and caught lightning bugs. It was the perfect place to grow up—until May 2004, when my dad learned he was being deployed with his National Guard unit to Iraq.

At the time Dad wasn't sure that my mom, who worked full time, and my brother and I (just teenagers) would be able to handle the chores while he was away. We sold the cattle, most of our equipment and our home—but kept our horses and our loyal Australian shepherd, Otis. We ended up buying a 140-acre chunk of land closer to town that was easier to handle.

When Dad returned, we bought a small herd of Angus cattle and began to rebuild. I went to college in 2007. In 2011, I married Seth Connell, an Army veteran who had served two tours in Iraq. We bought my parents' 140-acre place. We have a dog, Stubby, and we home-school our three children—Lance, Katie and Wyat. They help us with the daily tasks on our ranch, which has now grown to 460 acres.

We are proud to use innovative farming methods. One of them is a solar-powered watering system (from Kelln Solar out of Canada) that draws water from lakes, rivers, streams and ponds. The system uses a solar panel hooked up to a battery inside a waterproof tote. We position these near the water source, then connect a floating pump to the battery and a long hose. The hose runs away from the water source and sits above the water tank in order to fill it. A float connected to the battery tells it when to turn on or shut off the water flow.

This watering system keeps cattle away from the water source, so they don't destroy the surrounding ground and plant life, and won't foul stagnant water. The system uses a renewable resource to operate, is easy to set up and is very portable. We were the first ones in the state to utilize it.

In addition to ranching and raising three children, I've written a cookbook

called *The Ranch Woman's Cook Book*, as well as two series of contemporary romances and several stand-alone books, including *The Homeschool Way: A How To Guide to Homeschooling.*

EQUIPMENT WOES & GARDEN WORK

July 1 It rained all morning, so we visited our butcher and picked up a pig for the freezer. By 1 p.m. the sun was shining and we began rebuilding a fence for a horse pasture. Seth and I used the skid loader and post pounder attachment to drive in some posts before stringing out the wire. The garden came next.

Our kids weeded, Seth tilled the pathways and I harvested veggies. We froze kale, kohlrabi and peas, and had the lettuce with our supper.

July 2 We hauled round bales home from our rented hay ground, then roamed the entire property searching for a lost calf. Turned out the little bugger was sleeping in a depression surrounded by

Left: Innovative farming methods and good old-fashioned teamwork are keys to the Connell family's success. Above: Rachel saddles up to ride.

Rachel and Seth married in 2011 and have been farming together ever since.

tall grass. He hopped up and ran right to his momma as soon as we got close.

July 4 Yesterday we cultivated corn all morning and cut hay all afternoon. But today is Independence Day and my birthday! Seth and the kids bought me a new cinch for my saddle and an ice cream cake. We baled all afternoon before it rained.

July 5 By 8 a.m. it was 80 degrees and humid. The kids and I decided to get as much gardening done as we could before it got hotter. We tilled pathways, weeded carrots, mounded potatoes and harvested snap peas. Later we went to the lake to cool off. Seth cultivated another field of corn that we'll eventually chop into silage to feed to our cattle through winter.

July 6 We got up a little earlier than usual to catch six of our bulls and put them out with the girls on our rented pastures. While Seth had a chiropractor appointment, Wyat, Katie and I weeded beans and tomatoes and Lance trapped gophers in the cornfields. The afternoon was all about equipment. We dropped off

a tractor tire that needed repairs and then made a parts run for a new AC compressor for our John Deere. Upon discovering a leak in the skid loader's hydraulic system, Seth and Lance spent a few hours figuring out where it was and how to fix it.

July 7 Today I got covered in tractor grease, hydraulic oil, cow poop, calf poop, dirt and sweat. My day began with putting the repaired tire back on the tractor and bunching bales so they could be hauled out. The semitrailer got three flats in the field, so we had to bring them over to our tire guy. Then we tore into the skid loader to continue looking for the leak. We found it, but the new hose won't get here until this Thursday.

Next we took apart the tractor's AC compressor, replaced the broken parts, flushed the system and drove the tractor to a mechanic to have the whole system vacuumed and the coolant replenished.

We ended the day by catching the last 13 late calvers. Six of the cows had finally calved and one cow was apparently open (not pregnant), so those seven were caught in the chute and worked, and the calves tagged and doctored. We hauled them to pasture a few miles away.

DOCTORING LIVESTOCK

July 8 After awakening to a tornado warning, we spent the next 45 minutes hanging out in the basement until the all-clear. After chores I drove Seth in to pick up his tractor and then we bought a roll of wire for the fence. I spent an hour updating cattle records—shots and medicine serial numbers—and getting calf information loaded into the computer.

July 9 Today I ran to Fleet Farm and bought more hydraulic oil for the skid loader. Then after I got home, Seth and I finished stringing fence wire and hanging gates. You should have seen how happy the mares were when I let them into that pen. They ran, bucked and rolled in the grass.

July 10 My yard has become a jungle, and the barnyard is even worse. It's time to mow the grass and whack some weeds. The garden needs some work, too. We have to mound the potatoes again and tie up the tomatoes some more since they have grown at least 6 inches. This is a never-ending summer process—most likely we'll spend every other day in the garden from here on out.

July 11 We got up with the sun today, intending to give cows booster shots and Ultra Boss bug pour-on. We discovered that Seth's horse, Rosie, had a nasty hoof-shaped cut on her forehead.

So while Seth saddled my horse, Star, and Lance's horse, Thunder, I got my Young Living Animal Scents ointment (this is the only ointment I will ever use). I also grabbed some peroxide and a bucket of Betadine mixed in warm water so I could clean the wound. It wasn't as bad as we'd thought. With a few weeks of care, Rosie will be good as new.

Eventually we loaded up the horses and went to the first pasture. The cows weren't far from where we had set up the Rawhide portable panel and chute system, but they were in the swampy side, so we had to ride through the muck to get them out. Within 15 minutes we had the herd caught; it took another hour to work through the group. Each cow and calf was given Ultra Boss; calves also got Synovex calf implants to boost their weight gain.

After finding a leak in the skid loader's hydraulic system, Seth and Lance dig in to figure out where it's coming from and how best to fix it.

The second pasture is about 30 minutes away, and it wasn't nearly as muddy. Star didn't know what to think about the sheep in the next pasture over. It was the first time she'd ever seen such creatures, but she did well—only a bit of sidestepping and flinching before we hurried after the cows. After working the cattle through the chute, the kids and I rode the horses back around the pasture to get out through the gate. Wyat rode Shadow, the tallest horse we own (16.2 hands). He had the biggest grin on his face by the time we reached the trailer.

July 13 The kids and I checked on late calvers and cleaned Rosie's wound. After lunch we loaded sheep panels to haul to a friend. We finally got the new part for the skid loader and spent a few hours fighting to get it in. Thank God it's fixed!

July 14 It rained all morning, so I did office work, which included checking in with my web designer about the progress of my new author website. When the sun came out, we used the skid loader to pick up wood poles and fence posts from the horse pasture's torn-out fence. Dad came over to haul the skid loader to his house to work on some of his fences.

FARM BUREAU BUSINESS

July 15 Seth, Wyat, Katie, Lance and I headed to our last pasture—about 90 minutes away—to work with the biggest portion of our herd. Halfway there, the right brake on the truck locked and we smelled something burning. We stopped

Above left: The Connells' horses have it good, with plentiful pasture. Above right: Katie helps out with horse grooming.

just outside the nearest town and checked. It was bad. We babied the truck and trailer across town to a mechanic, where the kids and I unloaded our horses and tied them to the trailer while Seth unhooked the truck and drove it into the shop. We spent two hours waiting in the trailer's shade. One caliper and brake line replacement later, we were finally on the road home. It turned out that while we were stuck, my dad caught and worked all the cows and calves on his own. He's pretty amazing.

July 16 Our ninth anniversary! The kids went to my parents' house for the weekend. Seth and I drove to Sioux Falls, South Dakota, to attend a two-day Farm Bureau meeting.

July 17 The weekend was quiet. We met with members of Minnesota's and South Dakota's Young Farmers & Ranchers (YF&R) committees. Then we toured a fire equipment company, Stockyards Ag Experience (which offers interactive farm-to-table exhibits) and Falls Overlook Cafe, which serves farm-fresh food.

July 18 We spent the morning in a joint state Farm Bureau meeting, where we planned next January's Leadership, Education, Advocacy and Promotion (LEAP) conference. Then we met with our YF&R state committee and had a working lunch before heading home.

July 19 My brother-in-law Tom Burke, a trained farrier, did horse hooves for us

this morning. He brought along his kids, Paige and Aiden, and they stayed a few more hours to play. My 2-year-old nephew, Clay, my brother's son, was dropped off to join in the fun. Katie and Paige washed and dehydrated vegetables, and Seth went to the hayfield with my dad to rake and bale. While the kids were occupied, I updated cow records and doctored a few cows that had hoof rot and pinkeye.

July 20 Since we were gone over the weekend, the house was in dire need of cleaning. While Katie and Lance helped an older neighbor with yardwork, Wyat helped at home with dishes, laundry and vacuuming.

July 21 It rained half the night, so all the hay Dad cut yesterday was too wet to rake or bale. Instead we weeded and harvested a gallon of cucumbers, two 5-gallon buckets of green beans, and a wheelbarrow full of zucchini and eggplants. I also checked on the corn we had planted for silage and made a deal with a friend to trade vegetables for processed, packaged and frozen chickens.

BALING HAY, COWS ON THE LOOSE

July 22 I woke up early to saddle horses for Seth, our kids, my parents and me. We drove to the closest pasture and herded cows into the Rawhide. Two cows needed some medicine for hoof rot. When we got home, Katie and Lance cleaned the barn

and Seth went to load bales onto the semi for my dad to haul.

Wyat cleaned his disaster of a room (I swear he lets piglets loose in there), and I dehydrated onions. I also boxed up extra vegetables to take to my friend, who will have chickens ready for me to pick up on Friday.

July 23 I followed Seth to the hayfield after his Farm Bureau Zoom call so he could leave the baler there and I could bring him home. Later I prepared the kids' study space for when our fourth year of home-schooling starts in two weeks.

July 24 I drove to our farthest pasture to fix fences; the owner said cows had been out in her oat field the day before. I put salt and mineral out for the late calvers that are still at the house. The vet confirmed they're pregnant but, boy, are they late!

July 25 The boys cut hay and raked and baled the hay that was already down. I worked on a reading lesson with Wyat and got laundry done so everyone would have some clean clothes for our three-day Farm Bureau trip that starts tomorrow.

July 26 We drove four hours for a state Farm Bureau board of directors meeting. (My parents agreed to take care of the farm.) The kids hated every minute, and I don't blame them. I'm not a fan of being cooped up in a vehicle for that long either.

July 27 We spent today on sightseeing, education and field tours. We ate dinner at a board member's farm, but the meal came from a food truck since everyone had missed out on fair food this year. Tomorrow I'll attend a board of directors meeting and then we'll head home.

July 29 Equipment problems! A bearing went out on the baler yesterday, so Seth hauled it to the mechanic to get it fixed. Then the rake needed a few teeth replaced. Dad showed up to haul out the last four cows that have not calved yet and may not be pregnant after all. Unfortunately, his trailer had a flat when he arrived.

July 30 A friend phoned to let me know that our cows were out near the highway. Not a good call to get! I called Seth, who was helping his parents, and he raced over to get the cows back in. He found the gate wide open and truck tracks in our hayfield leading up to the gate. It's the second time this has happened this year.

July 31 It's the final day of a chaotic, busy month. The guys will be back soon with the last of the hay, and then I'm off to buy our groceries for next month.

For now I'm planning next summer's road trip to South Dakota, Wyoming, Colorado and Utah. We plan to revisit Mount Rushmore, the Crazy Horse Memorial, the Days of '76 Rodeo, Reptile Gardens and Bear Country USA. We'll also see places we've never been, such as Dinosaur National Monument and Mesa Verde National Park. Can't wait!

Rachel, herding cattle, grew up farming and still works closely with her dad, who maintains a farm nearby.

TRAILBLAZERS

Meet three women whose passion for horses led them on paths honoring the legacy of the Black cowgirls before them.

CHANDRA THOMAS WHITFIELD DENVER, COLORADO

The Hollywood image of the American cowboy is pretty consistent: a booted man in a wide-brimmed hat, riding horseback and effortlessly lassoing cattle, wrangling rambunctious bulls or galloping across rough terrain. He is rugged, strong, brave and most likely a white man.

In the days of the Old West, though, Black cowboys made up an estimated one-quarter of America's wranglers, riders and ropers. Black women were a part of that rich history, too. They rode horses and worked the land on ranches and farms at a time when their humanity was often challenged and the laws were not on their side. Many endured blatant gender and racial discrimination and exclusion in the world of competition. Still, they pressed on with their passion, pursuing opportunities to partake in daring equestrian escapades of their own.

Their contributions are not lost among a small but equally passionate group of modern Black women—cowgirls of color who hope to help illuminate the legacy left by their foremothers. Many of them say that they dream of a day when diverse representation will be celebrated in this sport still primarily dominated by men.

BRITTANEY LOGAN

Some years ago, Brittaney Logan was a city girl who didn't know a thing about riding horses. In fact, she says she was just being polite when she agreed to mount one while visiting a ranch owned by a friend, a competitive bronco rider active in the Black cowboy community.

"He basically put me on a horse, and I fell in love right then and there," says Brittaney, whose friends call her Britt Brat. "And ever since then, I've been riding horses."

After completing some training, she went on to become one of the founding members of the Cowgirls of Color, an all-female competition group of Black women from the Washington, D.C., and Maryland areas. In 2016, they made a name for themselves in the relay team competition at the Bill Pickett Invitational Rodeo, the nation's only touring Black rodeo, and went on to win third place in the category in 2019. The group has now disbanded, but Brittaney says she plans to continue competing—no small feat considering that she nearly lost her life in a riding accident in May 2020. During a trail ride, her horse's hoof slipped on some rocks while it was jumping out of a small creek, and the horse fell on her.

"So, my horse crushed six of my ribs and my lungs collapsed while I was still underwater," she says. She was rushed to a hospital, where she underwent an emergency surgery. During her ongoing recovery, Brittaney—who also competed in barrel racing and had been training as a mounted shooter before the onset of the pandemic—has taken up gardening and restoring furniture for fun.

"I didn't want to be in a depressed state because I couldn't ride my horse," she says. "There was COVID, and I was in pain, so to avoid depression, I just had to concern myself with something."

Brittaney says she looks forward to competing again once the COVID-19

threat subsides. She hopes her presence on the competition circuit will pay homage to Black cowgirls who have paved the way, such as Sharon Braxton (see page 63). She also hopes to inspire more Black women to bring their "Black girl magic" to the sport.

"We're not just prissy, we're not just scared to get our hair wet. We're not like the stereotype out there of Black women who don't like to be outdoors and things like that," she says. "It's definitely a good thing to bring exposure to that!"

Brittaney Logan fell in love with horses about five years ago, and she has been riding and competing in rodeos ever since.

Studies have shown that reading to animals (which lend an ear and do not judge) can improve kids' literacy skills.

CAITLIN GOOCH

For as long as she can remember, North Carolina native Caitlin Gooch has loved riding horses and reading. In 2017 she created an organization that celebrates both. A dedicated leisure rider and rodeo relay race competitor, Caitlin learned of the startlingly low literacy rates among Black children in her home state and decided she needed to do something.

She approached the library in her hometown of Eagle Rock, North Carolina, about partnering on a reading incentive program. Children who checked out three or more books from the library each month could sign up to be entered into a drawing to win a free visit to the horse farm that Donal Gooch, Caitlin's dad, had built on the family's sprawling land in Eagle Rock.

The program took off, but when transportation challenges kept some winners from visiting the farm, Caitlin decided to take the books and horses to them. Her Saddle Up and Read program officially gained nonprofit status in April 2019.

Pre-pandemic, Caitlin—a married mother of three who now lives in Chesapeake, Virginia—hit the road a few times a month to read to and take donated books to kids at elementary schools, libraries, child care centers, church youth groups and community events across North Carolina.

She says she's become accustomed to the double takes, curious stares and questions (such as "Whose horse is this?") that usually pop up when she shows up at events. Caitlin, who's been riding since the age of 3, says, "I don't know how to not be a country girl." She presses on because of her passion for the work. "It's fun; I just love it," she says.

Her efforts have earned her numerous accolades, including shoutouts on social media from Oprah Winfrey, LeVar Burton of *Reading Rainbow* fame, Kelly Clarkson and Brad Paisley.

The slower pace during the pandemic has allowed Caitlin to spend more time focused on home-schooling her children and fundraising. She hopes her ongoing GoFundMe campaign will help her buy enough land in her hometown to build an equestrian center and library, which she envisions will serve as a positive space for kids in that area.

"In my hometown, there is not much of anything for kids to do," she says. "I believe that building this space for them to be exposed to horses and providing books with characters who look like them will help push Saddle Up and Read to raise literacy rates in North Carolina."

SHARON BRAXTON

You can't explore the contributions of Black cowgirls without trick rider Sharon Braxton's name coming up. As one of the first female African American barrel racers in the Women's Professional Rodeo Association, she secured her place in history as one of the most decorated Black cowgirls ever.

"I wanted to be a competitor," says Sharon of her heyday in the 1960s and 1970s. And that she became.

"She first dabbled in English horse riding to improve her 'core and seat,' but her true passion was turn-and-burn three-barrel racing," says Sharon's niece Michele Braxton-Nelson. "She would often compete in jackpot barrel racing in local arenas throughout California, and she even produced the 1983 Ebony and Ivory Rodeo at the Burbank Equestrian Center."

Over the course of her long 30-plus-year career, Sharon also awed audiences as the first—and only—female announcer at the Bill Pickett Invitational Rodeo and at the Frontier 101 rodeo.

Retired since 2000 and now living in Fontana, California, Sharon is a proud grandmother of five and has one great-grandson. She says her deep love for the sport has never diminished. The elation and joy she felt in her competition days remains unmatched. "I saw white girls riding, and I wanted to ride, too," she remembers. "I said to myself, 'If they can do it, I can do it, too.'"

A West Virginia native, she headed to Southern California in the late 1960s as a single mom to take a job with the Pacific Bell phone company. She bought a horse with her first paycheck—and the rest, as they say, is history.

Sharon was presented with the first annual Trail Blazer lifetime achievement award at the G Look Cowboy Ball in 2019 for her many contributions to the equine industry. She attributes much of her career success to the soulful connection

she's always shared with animals, especially her horses.

"They're massive animals, but they really are kindhearted if you treat them the right way," she says of her horses. "They respond to kindness; you get more out of them through being kind than through abusing them and forcing them, as some people do."

Sharon says she misses competing, but she now enjoys mentoring young talent, including Michele. "Don't be discouraged; we all have our good and bad days," she tells younger Black women aspiring to follow in her footsteps. "You've got to keep moving forward—because if you give up, then you've lost."

Sharon Braxton spent her rodeo career as a barrel racer and has since gone on to inspire generations of young riders.

PURVEYORS OF POULTRY AND PRESERVES

This tiny shed has a lot to offer passersby.

KATHIE ROTHKOP NOVATO, CALIFORNIA

When Marie Reis' neighbor Debra Friedrichsen Shaw asked her to provide a few jars of homemade preserves for Debra's local farm stand in Petaluma, California, Marie says she figured, "Why not?" She'd been off work for three months while a broken elbow healed, and it was an opportunity to put a little extra cash into her pocket.

She started with a dozen jars of her "simple" jams, such as apricot and blackberry. The preserves resonated with Debra's customers, and the test paid off. "When I made my first $7, I was so excited that I drove into town and spent it on a triple latte!" Marie recalls.

Debra, a third-generation poultry farmer, had been stocking her tiny Farm Barn stand with eggs from her 53 ducks and 2,700 chickens. (She also sells eggs at a local farmers market.) "I felt there was a need for the community to appreciate the taste of a good fresh egg," she says.

Looking to increase options for her customers, she reached out to Marie. "Her offerings give customers more reason to shop," she says. "Marie recently put in a 'take a book, leave a book' box, too. It gets a lot of attention."

The arrangement between the two neighbors has been fruitful. Marie has branched out to other products—Meyer lemon vanilla-bean marmalade, fig pecan port cherry jam, quince habanero jam, chipotle apple butter and spicy pickled carrot sticks. "Anything spicy tends to fly off the shelf," Marie says. "This project has catered to my creative side and made me think outside the box. I love sharing my recipes with the public."

The work has paid off in other ways, too. "I saved all my money from the Farm Barn last year and put a down payment on a new car," Marie says. It's a long way from a triple latte.

Debra runs the stand on the honor system, so customers—many of them tourists driving through California's wine country—show their appreciation in the form of little notes. "I had a message the other day from a customer saying, 'Hooked on pickled carrot sticks! Please make more!'" Marie says.

Customer notes are a favorite part of the job for Debra, too. "I love reading our guest book," she says. "People leave all kinds of sweet thoughts and tell us why they love visiting our stand. One woman took a picture of one of my hens, which had sneaked into the Farm Barn and was sitting on the shelf. She left the photo for me on her next visit."

Above: Debra Friedrichsen Shaw with some of her 2,700 chickens. Left: The Farm Barn gave Marie Reis (pictured at right) reason to experiment with new preserves recipes.

Scrapbook

CAPTURE THE BEAUTY AROUND YOU

2

1. MAJESTIC MOUNTAINS
A horse grazes beneath the Grand Teton mountain range in Wyoming.
KATARINA BATES YORBA LINDA, CA

2. DRIFTING AWAY
My son Cameron paddles the waters off Cape Hatteras National Seashore at sunset.
CORY FICK SHILLINGTON, PA

1. TAKE IT FROM THE TOP

The Havasupai Indian Reservation in Arizona features three main waterfalls. Mooney Falls, the tallest at 190 feet, is my favorite.

GRANT CLOUD WHITELAND, IN

2. SCENIC PAWS

Our mini dachshunds, Bea Taylor and Thelma Lou, admire the view from the Sunset Rock overlook in Highlands, North Carolina.

HOLLIE CARTLEDGE MOBILE, AL

3. PAYING RESPECTS

Our family volunteers every year to place flags on veterans' graves. I took this photo as ROTC cadets passed our youngest daughter, Madison.

GERRY EISERT PAPILLION, NEBRASKA

1. HANDMADE BLOCKS

My barn quilt blocks were featured on a trail in Pennsylvania. My husband and I handmade them. It was one of our more fun projects.

LEE HART MEADVILLE, PA

2. ON POPS' POND

Joe Zielinski, known as Pops to his grandkids, shares the bounty of his pond with his grandson Morgan, 12, who caught a bass there.

AMY WILER O'FALLON, MISSOURI

3. BIRD AND BLOOM

I took this photo in the McKee-Beshers Wildlife Management Area in Maryland. The state plants sunflowers to attract wildlife for the fall hunters, but we get to enjoy the flowers and birds during the brief peak of fantastic yellow in July. An amazing variety of birds land in the fields. It is a photographer's dream come true!

JANE GAMBLE ALEXANDRIA, VIRGINIA

WET WEATHER WONDER
After being stuck in our tent most of the day because of rain at Lake Elmo Park Reserve in Minnesota, my daughters and I emerged to see a beautiful reflected rainbow.

JULIE HOLM COTTAGE GROVE, MN

1

1. PEEKABOO
This shy friend was keeping close to its mama at Beefmaster Breeders in Texas.

DAVID R. STOECKLEIN BOZEMAN, MONTANA

2. HAPPY TO SEE YOU
This reminds me of a bunch of kids peeking around each other to see what is going on. I love sunflowers, and yellow is such a happy color.

TERRY CRANK SEDGEWICKVILLE, MISSOURI

3. PREHISTORY COMES ALIVE
My kids (from left: Dakota, Savannah and Austin) get close to a T. rex in the Utah desert.

KATHLEEN WAITSCHIES OAK HILLS, CALIFORNIA

2

1. SMOOTH SAILING
Lifetime collections of antiques help bring a Northeast nautical look to a West Coast home.

KELLY HIKIDA, IRVINE, CA

2. KITTY ON THE CASE
My sister Becky took this guy's photo on her ranch in Ontario, Canada, where he helps keep the mouse population down.

BRENDA HANSEN CLINTONVILLE, WISCONSIN

3. MEMORIES THAT LAST
Bridal Veil Falls is one of the most beautiful sites in Yosemite National Park. I camped in the park as a child, later on with my children, and now with my grandchildren.

JANET SCHMIDT VACAVILLE, CA

1. EXPLORING THE GREAT OUTDOORS

Rock Island State Park, a 912-acre primitive island in Lake Michigan off the tip of Door County peninsula, is my favorite place in the world. Here, my daughter Tansy Lederhaus paddles along the rugged cliffs of the western shore.

TIM SWEET APPLETON, WI

2. WASHINGTON OAKS GARDENS STATE PARK

On my adventures though Washington Oaks Gardens State Park I came upon this great blue heron by a bait station. I do believe this bird could read. It was as if he knew more bait was on the way.

WALT MATHER NEW WOODSTOCK, NY

3. SHOWING THE WAY

Lights inside one of the few remaining fire lookouts in our state (this one is in Ouachita National Forest) made the tower look like a beacon pointing to the dark, starry skies above.

BRENNEN DUFFIELD RUSSELLVILLE, ARKANSAS

Heart & Soul

A LONG TIME COMING

Stints in the tomato business brought two men together as friends in retirement.

JOHN C. MATTHEW BOISE, IDAHO

Hugh Newcomb and I met in 2015, after we moved into the same retirement community in Boise, and it wasn't long before we discovered that we had something in common: Years earlier, we had both worked in the Indiana tomato industry.

From the start, it was clear that Hugh was a true storyteller. In fact, he wrote remembrance columns for several small newspapers in his home state and had written a book, *A Collection of Stories out of Arkansas*. We had lunch together often, and through sharing stories of our rural pasts, our friendship grew.

In 1945, Hugh was a 15-year-old student looking to earn some money to save for his college education. He traveled north with a friend to work on a farm that was near Markle, not far from Fort Wayne. At the time, I was an 18-year-old high school graduate in vocational agriculture, just taking over my family's Madison County farm—a typical 160-acre operation. That same year I planned to grow 10 acres of tomatoes for a 4-H project and to earn money for college.

In those years, there was a strong connection between our respective states' farming communities, since most of the pickers for the Indiana tomato harvest were recruited from Arkansas. How neat to learn that my new friend had come to pick tomatoes during the same summer that I was growing them!

Baskets of farm-fresh tomatoes on the flatbed of a truck are ready to go to market.

With World War II winding down, the John Deere Co. had restarted its tractor production, and I bought an almost-new John Deere B from a cousin who had been farming our land. As Hugh was anticipating his summer adventure and all the new riches that he might find as a tomato picker, I was preparing my fields for when another family of pickers would arrive from Arkansas.

I plowed, disked, added fertilizer and signed a contract with the Stokely-Van Camp cannery to buy and process my crop. They supplied tomato plants grown in Georgia—an open-pollinated variety called Baltimore, considered an heirloom nowadays. Baltimores would continue to grow throughout the summer, producing up to three pickings (and maybe a fourth if we didn't get an early hard freeze).

It was a late and wet spring when planting began that year, and we shared equipment and labor with neighboring growers. The cannery had provided a transplanter, which was pulled by a tractor. It had a blade that opened the furrow, a water tank on the back and two low seats on either side. The young and nimble among us had the "privilege" of riding in those seats and placing plants into the furrow just as the water tripped. Angled disks behind us pushed the soil back around the plants. It was a slow, dirty and tedious job.

When planting was done, I'd use my tractor to cultivate for weeds—much as you would for corn or soybeans—until the tomatoes began to vine. At that point it was time to get out the hoe and start carrying a sharpening file in my back pocket. When the time came to harvest in August, we used a pitchfork to turn over the vines about every 20 rows, making roads for a truck or wagon.

We distributed some factory-supplied hampers for picking and loading; each held five-eighths of a bushel and weighed more than 30 pounds when full. For pay of 12 cents a load, the pickers moved through the field, filling their hampers and then setting them beside the road for collection. With help, I loaded those hampers onto my wagon (a half-ton International) or sometimes onto my neighbor's REO Speed Wagon—not to be confused with the rock band of the same name!

Red, ripe tomatoes are ready for harvesting..

We stacked the hampers in a staggered fashion, four or five rows high. After securing the top row, I'd drive to the cannery, unload the tomatoes and reload the empty hampers to take back to the field for the pickers to fill again.

With the wet weather that year, our tomatoes were of high quality, winning first place at the state 4-H fair. At the county 4-H fair, I won a sweepstakes ribbon for tomatoes. And then, at a county 4-H tomato and potato show, I was crowned 1945's Tomato King of Madison County.

At one time there were more than 100 tomato canneries in Indiana, but now there is just one family-owned processor, Red Gold, which is based in my home county. Yet Indiana is still among the largest producers of processed tomatoes in the States. Growers today plant Romas, which are tough enough to harvest mechanically and load onto trucks in bulk. It's a far cry from the way Hugh and I spent our summers in 1945.

Hugh died in 2020, but I'm so glad to have called him a friend. He and I always loved to wax nostalgic about our time harvesting Indiana tomatoes 75 years ago. And we both agreed that it was a story worth sharing.

SINGING HER PRAISES

His mother worked as hard in the kitchen as any man in the field.

DARWIN ANTHONY TRIMONT, MINNESOTA

The threshermen's meal wasn't just lunch. It was an event. There was a certain feeling of competition, too, with food that showed off the skills of the cook and grain yields that showed off the skills of the farmers.

My mother worked hard to plan and prepare these meals, and if the threshing wasn't completed the first day—because of a rain delay, heavy dew or larger-than-average yields—she would be expected to serve them up for two consecutive days.

She fired the cookstove with wood or corn cobs. To keep the heat at bay, our summer kitchen (where my mother also did laundry and canning) was located away from the main house.

The summers were hot, and we didn't have electricity, so we used a small icebox to keep things cool. These meals were a very important part of life on the prairie, and timing was crucial. The rush began long before noon—in addition to the midday meal, my mother also made a "morning lunch" of sandwiches that she delivered to the field.

This was well before the time of prepackaged food, so everything was made from scratch. The farm supplied meat—usually roast beef, pork or fried chicken—and the large garden provided vegetables. When she was done cooking, my mother would carry the prepared food to the house kitchen, where a hungry crew sat "washed and waiting."

The men washed in an enamel pan that sat on a bench near the windmill. They filled the pan from the "cooler," a small tank near the main stock tank. Each would wipe the sweat from his face and hands with towels my mother had made from feedsacks.

At the table the men passed around large platters, emptying them quickly. After piling their plates with meat and mashed potatoes, they'd pour on a rich gravy made with drippings from the pan and top it all off with string beans and peas. As they ate, the men talked of the weather, crop prices and horses. There was an unwritten rule that politics and religion were off-limits. At the end of the meal, my mother served homemade pie.

My mother was a wonderful cook, but few of the men ever remarked on the meal. For this reason, I will always remember our neighbor John Intlekoefer. He always thanked my mother. Receiving such a compliment was rare in those days, as most took her work for granted.

As the men got up from the table and moved outside, those who'd finished early might find some shade and lie on the lawn. Meanwhile, my mother set about washing the dishes, kettles and skillets before starting on the afternoon meal.

I am absolutely convinced that my mother worked harder than any of the threshermen, including my own father. But history speaks of the workers in the field—and not enough about the workers in the kitchens.

Minnesota threshermen in the 1930s worked hard.

Michael, who studied agriculture at Cornell before earning his Ph.D. in natural resources, shares some of that knowledge with a group of Hopi children taking part in one of their village's summer youth programs.

years," he says. "Our faith says to plant every year, and so we do."

Roughly one-third of Hopi residents farm, says Terri Honani, program manager for the Natwani Coalition, a nonprofit dedicated to preserving Hopi farming traditions. Fewer people plant, and fields are smaller than they once were, Terri says, but the Hopi people are still defined by agriculture.

"It's a lifestyle of growing, harvesting, preserving and cooking," she says. "Our teachings tell us to plant seeds and store the excess harvest to make sure that our families are prepared for things such as droughts or the COVID-19 pandemic."

The Hopi faced physical and cultural threats from the Spanish during the 16th century and from Christian missionaries during the 19th and 20th centuries. But the Hopi held tight to their ceremonies and culture, which both go hand in hand with agriculture.

"Our role has always been dry farming," Terri says. "The Creator told us we can live here as long as we're stewards of the land, so we've always held strongly to that. Our ceremonies and culture and language are still intact, and that has everything to do with our commitment to farming."

The agricultural calendar of the Hopi nation begins with a ceremony in February and ends in November after the harvest.

In late winter, Hopi women look over their reserves of corn and determine what colors and quantities to plant. Hopi men, both young and old, then work together in the fields, forming planting parties and using greasewood sticks to dig deep into the soil until they hit moisture. A handful of seeds is dropped into each hole, so the plants emerge in clusters, eventually yielding a variety of fresh melons and squash, as well as the many colors of corn (yellow, white, red, blue and purple) used in traditional ceremonies.

"The men get together and plant," Terri says. "The fields provide a place and time for the knowledge of planting to be passed from one generation to the next."

What works on Hopi land may not work elsewhere. "There is not a recipe or a cookie-cutter approach to dry farming," Amy says. "It requires a willingness to explore, to fail, to start small and learn from mistakes. You can't schedule what to do when. You have to pay attention, be present and observe the soil." This mindful approach to farming, sprouted

from necessity, is carving out a niche market for organically grown, dry-farmed produce that is gaining a reputation for enhanced flavor and texture. As climate change ravages the agriculture industry, more farmers are turning to the tried-and-true techniques used by indigenous people for generations.

At Oregon State University, Amy works with farmers across the Pacific Northwest and California who are seeking guidance as they explore options on land without

> **We chose this hard landscape to survive in, and our seeds have adapted. It's not an easy life, but it's rewarding."**

water rights and adapt to increasingly scarce water supplies for irrigation.

"With climate change, we're seeing less snowpack, which impacts streamflow and therefore water availability for irrigation for those with water rights," Amy says. "The less reliant we are on irrigation systems, the more resilient our food systems are going to be."

Michael, who helps educate others about the benefits of dry farming, works from his home on the Hopi nation. For him, coaxing life from the barren earth has little to do with economics.

"There's no separation between who I am and what I do," he says. "There's no separation between agriculture and ceremony. When a Hopi baby is 2 weeks old, he's raised to the east and given a piece of sweet corn pudding to tie him to his identity. It's a beautiful thing to watch, and it's ingrained in us as Hopi."

Top left: Michael is building a home using traditional materials, such as sandstone, and techniques the Hopi have used for over 2,000 years. Bottom left: Corn grows despite drought. Right: Corn is shucked and set outside for about a month to dry. It stays on the cob until the time of use and can be stored indefinitely.

WELL-MADE BEDS

Volunteers blanket animal shelters across the country with handcrafted comfort.

JILL GLEESON GLEN ELLYN, ILLINOIS

I t really all started with a kitten. Linda Kastiel Kozlowski, the founder of Comfort for Critters, was in her local animal shelter adopting the meowing ball of fuzz when she noticed all the rest of the homeless pets in their enclosures. She was helping one, but what could she do for the other 50 she couldn't take with her? Inspiration came when a shelter worker told her they sometimes lined the cages with old towels to make the animals more comfortable.

"I'm a Christian," Linda says, "and I felt a tap on my shoulder to do something about all these pets. I had been crocheting my whole life, so I said, 'How about I crochet blankets and you can use them instead of the old towels?' I was really answering a calling I had."

That first year, Linda (a busy mother of two, who also manages a custom drapery business) made about 50 blankets and gave them to the shelter free of charge. The shelter used them as cozy cage liners and then sent them home with newly adopted pets, providing something familiar as the pets adjusted to their new families.

Linda kept crocheting, and within a few years, she was donating her handiwork to six shelters around her hometown of Glen Ellyn, Illinois. Word of her good deeds spread locally.

After she put up the Comfort for Critters website, word quickly spread farther, even reaching across the country. People joined her in the mission—first in a trickle, then in a flood.

Fourteen years after she made her first blanket, Linda's organization boasts about 1,000 volunteers nationwide. They service shelters in every state—a total of around 400 by Linda's last count.

In 2020, Comfort for Critters provided 20,023 blankets made from donated yarn, all of them used to provide warm, soft

bedding for homeless pets—and all of them crafted by hand.

"We feel like making the blankets is really an exercise in love for the volunteers," Linda says. "They think about the pets in the shelter they'll be helping as they crochet, so they really pour themselves into it. It's turned out to be almost as big a blessing to the volunteers as it has the pets."

A stack of 233 blankets made by a Comfort for Critters volunteer measures nearly as tall as founder Linda Kastiel Kozlowski.

As a child in the 1940s, Jewell Johnson loved to visit her grandmother's farm, which was laid out in the same way as the one pictured here, with the house quite a distance away from the barn, the pig pen, the hen house and the pasture.

TO GRANDMOTHER'S FARM WE GO

For a kid from town, nothing stacked up to these thrilling summer visits.

JEWELL JOHNSON FOUNTAIN HILLS, ARIZONA

Every summer, Mom and I went out to Grandma's farm to help preserve her garden produce. We lived in town, so spending a week on the farm was an adventure for me.

With six cows to milk, chickens to feed and hogs to slop, Grandma had little time to plan elaborate meals. For breakfast she served oatmeal. Because I was a picky eater, I would skip this course. At noon we had boiled potatoes and fried side pork. We never had any desserts or salads; the vegetables we preserved were to be saved for winter meals. In the evening, we ate fried potatoes and side pork again.

Bedtime was at sundown—with no electric lights, why waste money burning kerosene? Both Mom and I slept on straw mattresses that Grandma had made by hand. The straw crunched every time I turned over, so it took some time to get to sleep. And Grandma's farm had geese— large gray geese with wingspans of about 5 feet. Each time I went to the outhouse, they seemed to be there waiting, hissing, flapping their wings. My heart hammered, and I would be breathless by the time I finally slammed the outhouse door. We didn't have such creatures in town—or such excitement!

But my favorite time on the farm was in the late afternoon when Grandma, Fido the dog and I went into the meadow to bring the cows in for milking. As we walked along in the lush pasture grass, Grandma called, "Here, boss! Here, boss!" When we saw the cows, Fido bounded after them, herding them to the barn.

For an 8-year-old town girl, nothing could compare to ambling in the sweet-smelling meadow on a summer afternoon with Grandma.

Taste of the Country

TROPICAL BBQ CHICKEN

PREP 15 min. **COOK** 3 hours
MAKES 2 servings

- 2 chicken leg quarters (8 oz. each), skin removed
- 2 Tbsp. ketchup
- 3 Tbsp. orange juice
- 2 Tbsp. brown sugar
- 1 Tbsp. red wine vinegar
- 1 Tbsp. olive oil
- 1 tsp. minced fresh parsley
- ½ tsp. Worcestershire sauce
- ¼ tsp. garlic salt
- ⅛ tsp. pepper
- 2 tsp. cornstarch
- 1 Tbsp. cold water

1. With a sharp knife, cut leg quarters at joints if desired; place in 1½-qt. slow cooker. In a small bowl, combine the ketchup, orange juice, brown sugar, vinegar, olive oil, parsley, Worcestershire sauce, garlic salt and pepper; pour over chicken.

2. Cover and cook on low until chicken is tender, 3-4 hours.

3. Remove chicken to a serving platter; keep warm.

4. Skim fat from the cooking juices. Transfer ½ cup of the juices to a small saucepan; bring to a boil. Combine the cornstarch and water until smooth; gradually stir into pan. Bring to a boil; cook and stir until thickened, about 2 minutes. Serve sauce with chicken. If desired, top with additional fresh parsley.

1 SERVING 301 cal., 14g fat (3g sat. fat), 83mg chol., 601mg sod., 18g carb. (14g sugars, 0 fiber), 25g pro.

ALABAMA WHITE BBQ SAUCE

TAKES 5 min. + chilling **MAKES** 3 cups

- 2 cups mayonnaise
- 1 cup cider vinegar
- 2 Tbsp. pepper
- 2 Tbsp. lemon juice
- 1 tsp. salt
- ½ tsp. cayenne pepper

In a medium bowl, whisk all ingredients. Refrigerate 8 hours. Brush sauce over meat, chicken or veggies the last few minutes of grilling, or serve on the side.

2 TBSP. 124 cal., 13g fat (2g sat. fat), 1mg chol., 192mg sod., 1g carb. (0 sugars, 0 fiber), 0 pro.

ASPARAGUS TUNA NOODLE CASSEROLE

PREP 20 min. **COOK** 5 hours
MAKES 8 servings

- 2 cups uncooked elbow macaroni
- 2 cans (10½ oz. each) condensed cream of asparagus soup, undiluted
- 2 cups sliced fresh mushrooms
- 1 medium sweet red pepper, chopped
- 1 small onion, chopped
- ¼ cup lemon juice
- 1 Tbsp. dried parsley flakes, divided
- 1½ tsp. smoked paprika, divided
- 1 tsp. garlic salt
- ½ tsp. pepper
- 2 lbs. fresh asparagus, cut into 1-in. pieces
- 2 pouches (6.4 oz. each) light tuna in water
- 1½ cups shredded Colby cheese
- 1 cup multigrain snack chips, crushed
- 4 bacon strips, cooked and crumbled

1. Cook macaroni according to package directions for al dente; drain. Transfer to a 4- or 5-qt. greased slow cooker. Stir in soup, mushrooms, red pepper, onion, lemon juice, 1½ tsp. parsley, 1 tsp. paprika, garlic salt and pepper. Cook, covered, on low 4 hours.

2. Stir in asparagus and tuna. Cook, covered, on low until the asparagus is crisp-tender, about 1 hour longer. Sprinkle with remaining 1½ tsp. parsley and ½ tsp. paprika. Serve casserole with shredded cheese, crushed chips and crumbled bacon.

1⅓ CUPS 338 cal., 15g fat (6g sat. fat), 44mg chol., 1110mg sod., 30g carb. (5g sugars, 5g fiber), 22g pro.

WATERMELON BOMBE DESSERT

TAKES 20 min. + freezing
MAKES 8 servings

About 1 pint lime sherbet
About 1 pint pineapple sherbet
About 1½ pints raspberry sherbet
  ¼ cup miniature semisweet
       chocolate chips

1. Line a 1½-qt. bowl with plastic wrap. Press thin layer of slightly softened lime sherbet against the bottom and sides of the bowl. Freeze, uncovered, until firm. Evenly spread a thin layer of slightly softened pineapple sherbet over lime sherbet layer. Freeze, uncovered, until firm. Pack raspberry sherbet in center of sherbet-lined bowl. Smooth the top to resemble a cut watermelon.

2. Cover and freeze until firm, about 8 hours. To serve, uncover bowl of molded sherbet. Place a serving plate on bowl and invert. Remove bowl and peel off wrap.

3. Cut the bombe into 8 wedges; press a few chocolate chips into raspberry section of each wedge to resemble watermelon seeds.

1 WEDGE 205 cal., 4g fat (2g sat. fat), 8mg chol., 60mg sod., 43g carb. (35g sugars, 0 fiber), 2g pro.

NUTTY CHICKEN SANDWICHES

PREP 20 min. + chilling
MAKES 16 tea sandwiches

  1 **cup shredded cooked
       chicken breast**
  1 **hard-boiled large
       egg, chopped**
  ½ **cup unsweetened crushed
       pineapple, drained**
  ⅓ **cup mayonnaise**
  ½ **tsp. salt**
  ⅛ **tsp. pepper**
  ¼ **cup chopped
       pecans, toasted**
  ½ **cup fresh baby spinach**
  8 **slices white bread,
       crusts removed**

1. In a small bowl, combine the chicken, egg, pineapple, mayonnaise, salt and pepper. Cover and refrigerate at least 1 hour.

2. Just before serving, stir in pecans. Divide spinach among 4 slices of bread; top with chicken salad and remaining bread. Cut each sandwich into quarters, making 4 tea sandwiches.

1 TEA SANDWICH 103 cal., 6g fat (1g sat. fat), 19mg chol., 178mg sod., 9g carb. (2g sugars, 1g fiber), 4g pro.

CHOCOLATE CHIP STRAWBERRY ICE CREAM

PREP 25 min.
BAKE 15 min. + freezing
MAKES 1½ qt.

- 1⅔ cups sugar
- 5 Tbsp. cornstarch, divided
- 4 cups 2% milk
- 2 large egg yolks
- 1⅓ cups heavy whipping cream
- ⅔ cup half-and-half cream
- 3 tsp. vanilla extract
- ¼ cup light corn syrup
- 3 cups fresh strawberries, hulled
- 1 dark chocolate candy bar (8 oz.), finely chopped
- Optional: Whipped cream and maraschino cherries

1. In a large heavy saucepan, whisk the sugar with 4 Tbsp. cornstarch until blended; whisk in the milk until smooth. Bring to a boil, stirring constantly; cook and stir until thickened, 1-2 minutes. Reduce heat to low. In a small bowl, whisk a small amount of the hot mixture into the egg yolks; return all to pan, whisking constantly. Cook over low heat until mixture is thick and a thermometer reads 160°, 2-3 minutes, stirring constantly. Immediately remove from heat.

2. Quickly transfer to a large bowl, then place the bowl in a pan of ice water.

3. Stir gently and occasionally for 2 minutes, then stir in cream, half-and-half and vanilla. Press plastic wrap onto surface of custard. Refrigerate several hours or overnight.

4. Fill cylinder of ice cream freezer two-thirds full; freeze according to manufacturer's directions.

5. Meanwhile, place the remaining 1 Tbsp. cornstarch in a large skillet. Whisk in the corn syrup until smooth; add strawberries. Bring to a boil over medium heat; cook and stir until thickened, about 2 minutes. Mash strawberries; cool.

6. During the last 5 minutes of processing the ice cream, add the strawberry mixture and chopped chocolate. Transfer the ice cream to freezer containers, allowing headspace for expansion. Freeze at least 4 hours or until firm. If desired, serve with a dollop of whipped cream and a cherry.

½ CUP 397 cal., 19g fat (12g sat. fat), 76mg chol., 59mg sod., 56g carb. (50g sugars, 2g fiber), 6g pro.

PUFF PANCAKE WITH BOURBON PEACHES

PREP 20 min. **COOK** 20 min.
MAKES 6 servings

- 1 Tbsp. butter
- 3 large eggs, room temperature, lightly beaten
- ½ cup 2% milk
- 1 tsp. vanilla extract
- ⅛ tsp. salt
- ½ cup all-purpose flour
- 1 cup water
- 4 Tbsp. bourbon or peach nectar, divided
- 2 Tbsp. honey
- 2 Tbsp. peach preserves
- 3 cups sliced peeled peaches (about 5 medium) or frozen unsweetened sliced peaches

1. Preheat oven to 400°. Place butter in a 9-in. deep-dish pie plate; heat in oven until butter is melted, 2-3 minutes. In a bowl, whisk the eggs, milk, vanilla and salt until blended; then gradually whisk in flour. Remove pie plate from oven; tilt carefully to coat bottom and sides with melted butter. Immediately pour in egg mixture. Bake until puffed and browned, 18-22 minutes.

2. In a saucepan, combine the water, 3 Tbsp. bourbon, honey and preserves. Bring to a boil; reduce heat. Add peaches; cook and stir until peaches are tender, 3-4 minutes.

3. Remove peaches to a bowl; set aside. Bring sauce to a boil; cook and stir until sauce is reduced to ½ cup. Remove from heat; stir in the reserved peaches and remaining 1 Tbsp. bourbon.

4. Remove pancake from oven. Serve immediately with warm peach sauce.

1 SERVING 192 cal., 5g fat (2g sat. fat), 100mg chol., 110mg sod., 27g carb. (17g sugars, 1g fiber), 6g pro.

CHERRY LIMEADE

TAKES 10 min. **MAKES** 8 servings

- ¾ cup lime juice
- 1 cup sugar
- ½ cup maraschino cherry juice
- 2 liters lime carbonated water, chilled
- 8 maraschino cherries with stems
- 8 lime slices

1. In a large pitcher, combine lime juice and sugar. Cover and refrigerate.

2. Just before serving, stir maraschino cherry juice, carbonated water and ice cubes into lime juice mixture. Garnish with maraschino cherries and lime slices.

1 CUP 142 cal., 0 fat (0 sat. fat), 0 chol., 2mg sod., 39g carb. (31g sugars, 2g fiber), 0 pro

LAVENDER SHORTBREAD

PREP 45 min. + standing
BAKE 20 min. + cooling
MAKES about 4 dozen

- 2 cups confectioners' sugar
- 2 Tbsp. plus 2 tsp. finely snipped dried lavender flowers, divided
- 1 cup butter, softened
- ⅔ cup sugar
- 2 cups all-purpose flour
- ½ cup cornstarch
- ⅛ tsp. salt

1. In a bowl, combine the confectioners' sugar and 2 tsp. lavender; cover and set aside at room temperature for 24 hours.

2. In a bowl, cream butter, sugar and remaining 2 Tbsp. lavender. Combine flour, cornstarch and salt; add to the creamed mixture. Divide dough in half. Cover and refrigerate until easy to handle, about 2 hours.

3. Preheat oven to 325°. On a lightly floured surface, roll out 1 portion of the dough to ¼-in. thickness. Cut into 1½-in. squares. Place squares 1 in. apart on ungreased baking sheets. Prick with a fork several times. Repeat with remaining dough.

4. Bake until edges are lightly browned, 18-22 minutes. Cool 1 minute before removing to wire racks to cool completely. Sift reserved lavender sugar; discard lavender. Sprinkle cookies with the sugar. Store cookies in airtight containers.

1 COOKIE 88 cal., 4g fat (2g sat. fat), 10mg chol., 37mg sod., 13g carb. (8g sugars, 0 fiber), 1g pro.

The brilliant colors of fall fill Cascade Pass, inside North Cascades National Park in Washington State.

PHOTO BY INGE JOHNSSON

Autumn

The Good Life

A FULL HEART

The best parts of life in the country are the people who enjoy it with you.

LISA FIX RIDGEFIELD, WASHINGTON

Many changes have come to the Flying F Ranch—different owners, different crops and different livestock. But one thing remains constant—the amazing views of majestic Mount St. Helens to the northeast and Mount Hood to the southeast.

These often snow-covered peaks can be hidden during the rainy winter months, only to reappear on a clear blue day to help remind us how truly blessed we are. And sometimes a rainbow or two will accompany them.

This scenery became mine in April 2000 when I bought this 10-acre farm outside of Ridgefield, Washington. I work full time as a customer service director, and I raise beef cattle. I have a menagerie of animals, including chickens, horses and a crazy dog named Lambeau (a Green Bay Packers flag flies proudly in front of my house).

Around the Flying F there are charming farms and an area with boarding stables for horses. Three local wineries are located about a half-mile away (we're known for our pinot noir around here). This is my slice of heaven.

DREAM COME TRUE

The view is a constant reminder that my dream came true. As a child growing up in Green Bay, Wisconsin, I drew this place and colored it with crayons. I loved horses, wanted horses and had Breyer toy horses, but I lived in the city and having my favorite animal was not possible. One of our neighbors about six blocks away had a little barn with horses. I rode my bike there all the time to see and pet them.

> ❝ **With my entire family back in Wisconsin, this city girl had to learn a lot from her neighbors.** ❞

I packed a lunch, sat by the fence and just watched. I dreamed of owning a ranch with horses of my own someday and living in an old farmhouse. After 30 years, my wish finally came true.

The mountains definitely make this place magnificent, but so does the gift of being close to the land, helping friends and family, and celebrating with the community. Working on the ranch gives me an inner peace as nothing else can. Even when I am out gardening, bringing in hay or cleaning stalls, the place is magical to me. These simple tasks, so repetitive in nature, continually remind me to live and to appreciate all my blessings in life.

Each season has its own kind of beauty. In spring, often rain is falling one minute and then the sun starts shining the next. Everything grows like crazy with all that water, creating much greenery and a feeling of abundance.

Summer is my favorite time of the year, because the sun shines constantly and the days are long. My boyfriend, John, and I can enjoy riding horses after work or being in the garden for hours.

Autumn is fantastic, too. The changing of the seasons brings a copious amount of color—and pumpkins. And then the rainy winter brings with it a time to slow down on outdoor chores and relax during the holidays with friends and family. The winter season is also the time of year to plan for upcoming projects on the ranch—

Left: Lisa leads her step-grandson Jaedon and his dad, Andrew, on a pony ride. Above: Lisa's dog, Lambeau, just wants this calf to play.

how many cattle we will have, what vegetables we should plant and who is coming to visit.

GOOD NEIGHBORS

I didn't find just horses and the farm; I also found the amazing people in my small community.

With my entire family still back in Wisconsin, this city girl had to learn a lot from her neighbors and friends. I have the most incredible support system in the world. When my husband and I divorced, people pitched in to help me run the farm. They came here and did everything from taking down a tree to helping me buy cows (they also taught me to sort them).

On Dec. 5, 2005, the old barn burned down. The animals were safe, but I lost all the Christmas ornaments I had stored there. Word got out to my son's day care, and boxes of ornaments began showing up on my doorstep. Sometimes it is hard to believe that I'm here, surrounded by so many gracious and kind people.

Maybe what I've learned is that it's not about a place, after all, but about being a part of something bigger. When you can appreciate your community and the people in it, you have an opportunity to be special to each other—to be vulnerable when needing help, to show up to help when not asked, and to love people where they are in the moment. My heart is full.

Left: Lisa's grandson Armour looks cute in his cowboy hat. Above: Fall brings lots of pumpkins to the ranch.

FALL IN THE PARK

The tranquil beauty of autumn leaves are a balm to anyone who chooses to appreciate them.

ELAINE HEATH OMAHA, NEBRASKA

In autumn, my friend Charles Stoll and I visit Memorial Park in the Dundee neighborhood in Omaha, Nebraska. The park is a memorial to the veterans and service members of the U.S. armed forces who originated from or lived in Douglas County.

We purchase our supplies, pack our picnic lunch and blanket, then head for the great outdoors. We take a breather, enjoying the quietness and Mother Nature's calming effect.

Shaded by sunglasses, our meandering eyes are enticed by the glow of the orange, gold and red colors of the trees, which include aspen, birch, catalpa, elm, fir, maple, oak, pine and spruce, among many others. As Charles and I walk through the trees, we collect our thoughts and share our views with each other. Taking our time, we are aware of our surroundings, and feel exquisite contentment in this place and in life.

On this November day, we feel a slight breeze at our backs and the warmth of the sun's rays on our shoulders. We literally put up our feet and make ourselves at home among nature's beauty and serenity. We sit still and leisurely unwind from a harried week.

What a restful time this is, just to recline, lounge on a soft blanket and experience this paradise—an escape from our usual excessive busyness.

In Memorial Park, Charles and I find a serene environment, nature's ambiance and the sought-after colorful leaves of the graceful trees, which are exactly what we seek. In this casual, tranquil area filled with memories, we feel at peace.

Brent looks over a soybean field while discussing the excessive rains.

Wednesday and Thursday, and significant rain will end all our chances of planting canola this fall. While we plant only about 400 acres per year, growing zero canola next year would have a negative ripple effect for several years down the road. Plus, it looks like we'll see near-freezing temperatures on Saturday morning, and about 600 acres of our soybeans are not yet mature enough to withstand a frost. Freeze damage at this stage could easily reduce our yields by 50%.

With nothing to be done about weather, we all continued working around the shop. Terry finished cleaning the borrowed combine, and Zack drove the cleaned machine back to the neighbor's farm. I downloaded corn harvest data from the yield monitors for analysis.

Oct. 10 Weather continues to dominate our life on the farm. We received 0.2 inch of rain overnight and more throughout the day. Our early Saturday morning forecast arrived at 32 degrees with a chance of frost. Thankfully we have crop insurance, which can help lessen the blow of major damage, but it will still not fill the gap for us completely.

Every October we go over options for the following year with our seed provider. We need to place an order within the next few weeks to capture the best discounts and ensure we get our chosen varieties next spring. Zack and I spent most of the morning working out a seed plan.

Oct. 11 It's official: Our chance to plant canola this year is over. I loaded up the canola seed and made the hourlong drive to take it back to the dealer. Most seed companies allow farmers to return unused seed for a full refund. Half of my seed will go to someone elsewhere in the country who has run short. One farmer's loss is another's gain.

Oct. 12 It stayed just above freezing overnight, but there was a moderate frost at sunrise. All in all, we made it through this round with Mother Nature with minimal damage to the soybean crop.

Oct. 14 Terry took advantage of a little sunshine today to wrap up cleaning one of the combines. Then we brought the machine into our main workshop for the guys to get it ready for soybeans.

Oct. 15 Weird weather ruled the day. A light drizzle fell this morning, which was more inconvenient than rain. Zack and Greg worked on the broken combine. I sent Terry out to get started on a TLC barn repair job—one of those jobs that can be started or stopped midstream.

I met with our crop insurance adjuster today. He needed to take pictures of each unplanted field and verify the steps we took to prepare for planting. Afterward I continued evaluating corn yields and making seed decisions for next year.

Oct. 17 It finally dried up enough for Zack and Greg to start fieldwork ahead of planting wheat. I went to a Farm Service Agency committee meeting in town.

Oct. 18 The sun was shining, so it looked like a day to get fields ready for wheat. Greg headed out early to till up cornstalks. We plan to allow these fields to dry out over the weekend. They should be ready to fertilize and plant on Monday.

Oct. 19 Everyone got the day off. The first round of rain fell overnight, but was less than 0.1 inch so it will have no real impact on our plans.

Oct. 20 Today was a special Sunday with a bit of farm-related fun. One of the seed companies we work with sponsors a NASCAR driver. So the company gave us all tickets to the fall race at the Kansas Speedway, along with a few VIP goodies. I picked up Greg, Zack and Zack's son Nate at 6 a.m. to drive to the racetrack. Despite some morning fog, the weather was great for racing and we all had a good time.

Oct. 21 I dumped more than an inch of water out of the rain gauge this morning. Plans to start planting wheat this week were washed away, and the odds for us to plant any wheat this month are slim. Fortunately, most years we can plant wheat well into late November and still grow a decent crop.

WORKING WITH THE WEATHER

Oct. 22 Even though it was too wet for wheat, we had the soybeans—our major crop—standing in the fields. Zack evaluated them to figure out if the seed was dry enough and the ground was firm enough to drive across with the harvest equipment. We spent the rest of the morning getting the harvest equipment ready to go.

The summer weather was almost ideal for soybean development, so we were disappointed that harvest yields in this first field were only a little above average. We hope that the others will do better.

Oct. 23 Today was warm, sunny and very windy: a good day for harvesting soybeans. We harvested about 150 acres. Yields on these fields were a little better, so signs pointed to a good harvest. We knocked off earlier than usual because of the weather. There were strong winds today because of an approaching cold front that is expected to bring rain.

Oct. 24 Rain. I am as tired of putting it into this diary as you are of reading it. Overnight we got a slow 0.1 inch but it continued falling all day long. Slow, steady rains at this time of year fully saturate the soils even if the total amount is low. This will keep us out of the fields for at least another week. Any further major weather events in the next 10 to 15 days will almost certainly end fall planting before it starts.

Oct. 25 The showers yesterday and overnight brought us nearly 1 inch of rain, with more coming today. So we decided to put all the parts and other stuff gathered in our workshop back in order.

Greg continued his shop's electrical upgrade and finished everything that needed to be done inside. The shop's outside work can be done later in the winter after things dry up. Zack started another back-burner job—designing and building steel running-board steps for one of our pickup trucks. The existing ones have rusted away.

Oct. 29 Yesterday began with a slow, wet drizzle. Today it picked up the pace into rain showers. While doing office

Brent and Terry finish tightening the tracks on the combine.

work, I located a used articulated loader for sale that may be a good addition.

Oct. 30 Yesterday's rains brought another inch, but at least we've returned to just drizzle. The guys all worked in the shop while I drove to Tulsa to look at the loader. Everything about it matched my needs—a few signatures later and I became the proud owner of a new-to-me John Deere 344K loader.

Oct. 31 It was very cold, but the sun was shining. The soybean seed will be dry within the next few days, while it might easily take a full week for the ground to dry. Since we are so far behind with our harvest, we decided to swap out our largest combine's drive tires for rubber tracks. They'll provide a larger footprint to hold up the combine and will let us begin harvest as soon as the seed is ready.

While this sounds like an easy task, everything involved is big and heavy. Each combine track weighs more than 4,000 pounds, so we use our tractor with a front-end loader attachment to move them into position. After finishing the job, we spent the rest of the day making sure all the other harvest equipment is ready to go.

Postscript: What a month! We got a full 7 inches of rain, and 15 out of 31 days had water falling out of the sky. In row-crop farming, weather is the start, middle and end of every decision. Sometimes we work along with it, and other times we observe.

As frustrating as this month has been, we keep moving forward. Plans for next year are underway. Rendel Farms will go on, even when it rains.

RUGGED BEAUTY LIKE NO OTHER

In Texas' Great Plains region, the view is vast, the cattle roam freely and the land is treasured.

HANNAH CRANDALL EARTH, TEXAS

The Great Plains region of Texas may not receive quite as much recognition for its attractions as the state's more populated regions, but for those of us who call it home, we find beauty every day.

Whether in its history, people, landscape or seasons, there's something truly special about this place that sets it apart from the rest of the Lone Star State.

Located in the Texas Panhandle, the Great Plains stretch all the way to the border with New Mexico. Farming and ranching are the primary ways of life for most people in this area.

Because so much of this region is rural, it is pretty difficult to go farther than 30 miles without seeing herds of cattle. Drivers must often slow down for tractors on the highway, but these folks don't mind.

From windmills in the northern part of the region to oil rigs in the south, people here make a living off the land.

Small towns like my hometown of Earth (population 939) make the Great Plains of Texas all that it is. The people who reside in these communities have a deep respect for each other, as well as for where they live. Whether they live in a town with a population of 254,000 or 500, they are proud of where they come from. Everyone knows almost everyone else, but nobody is ever hesitant to welcome newcomers. I believe that this friendly feeling of community is the most beautiful thing in West Texas.

Seeing the sun rise and set from almost anywhere is an opportunity not everyone is blessed with. However, in this part of Texas, you can turn onto a dirt road and drive for miles while watching the sun in the distance. The peace and clarity that wash over you are almost indescribable. Over completely flat land or rolling hills, the sky is never hidden. The stars really are bigger and brighter in Texas, and it is especially obvious in these rural areas of the Great Plains.

Snow is absolutely beautiful here. My personal favorite is when there is just a light dusting across the open fields. The wind blows snow across the Plains with a

strength you'll find nowhere else, and the snowdrifts make snowy days even more fun for the kids.

Sure, the tumbleweeds caused by our West Texas wind can be a real pain, but in how many other places do you see tumbleweeds as tough as these?

Texas as a whole is an amazing state, but to be in the Great Plains region is something very special. The land and the way folks here care for it is truly extraordinary. Whether you come for a visit or a more permanent stay, the beauty you can find in the Panhandle of Texas is unlike any other.

Though the landscape of Texas' Great Plains can be dry at times, it has a rugged beauty that Hannah cherishes.

Scrapbook

CAPTURE THE BEAUTY AROUND YOU

1

2

1. WORTH THE TREK

I hiked the Mohonk Preserve Huguenot Trail on a sunny fall day up through the Labyrinth and Lemon Squeeze, a challenging maze of boulders, wooden ladders and narrow crevices. After climbing this hour-long trail, hikers are rewarded with sweeping views of the Catskill Mountains.

ALLYSA KAISER NEW YORK, NY

2. KODAK MOMENT

The Glade Creek Grist Mill in West Virginia's Babcock State Park is at its most beautiful when surrounded by autumn's colorful glory.

LILLIAN STEWART PRINCETON, WV

1. PERFECTLY POSED
I was traveling down the road one day and saw this gorgeous eagle surrounded by fall colors. I had to pull over and snap a photo.

SHERRY SANDERS MOUNTAIN HOME, AR

2. SPLENDOR AT SUNDOWN
My husband and I were on an overnight backpacking trip in Roan Mountain State Park here in Tennessee and made it to the summit of Grassy Ridge Bald (a mountain summit covered in grass) right as the sun set. It was quite a sight to behold!

ASHLEY JOHNSON JONESBOROUGH, TN

3. THERE OUGHT TO BE CLOWNS
Is a sloppy kiss from our Shorthorn show steer, Dilly, a trick or a treat? Our grandson Grady was glad to make a friend.

HOPE RICKER PITTSTON, MAINE

1. FEEDING TIME

This bear cub, deciding it was time to eat, cautiously waded out to his mom. This photo, taken in Katmai National Park and Preserve in Alaska, captures his begging eyes as he tries to get a bite in while his mother devours a freshly caught salmon.

MICHAEL BENSON TUCSON, ARIZONA

2. GRANDPA IS MY CO-PILOT

Raelyn and her Grandfather Tom love to spend time together. On this sunny fall day, they were hanging out on Grandpa's tractor, having a little visit.

JAMIE ROMINGER ZIONVILLE, NORTH CAROLINA

3. BRIDGE TO BEAUTY

Trough Creek State Park is one of Pennsylvania's best-kept secrets. We hiked, saw waterfalls and wildlife, and experienced nature.

ASHLY ASH NOTTINGHAM, PA

3

SUNRISE AT THE SUMMIT
My boyfriend and I hiked up Stowe
Pinnacle in Vermont and summited
around 5:30 a.m. We sat patiently in
the 20-degree weather and waited
for the rising sun.

CELYNN SIEMONS FAIRFAX, VT

1. HELLO, WORLD!

These Nubian dairy goats came to us at just 3 and 6 days old—so tiny that my toddlers could carry them with ease. Here they are on one of their first adventures exploring the farm.

AMBER BROMLEY SHERIDAN, MONTANA

2. PRESSING ON

Fresh apples are a sweet family legacy.

DANIELLE MILES MILLBURY, MASSACHUSETTS

3. WONDER GIRL

Kali is full of life, and Wonder Woman is her favorite character. She and her doll Lilly are ready for whatever adventures await!

NESA HARDEN CORAL SPRINGS, FLORIDA

1. SPOT THE DIFFERENCE
Such fun to share in my great-nephew Bradley's first autumn at his parents' place, Donaldson Farms.

KATIE DONALDSON
HACKETTSTOWN, NEW JERSEY

2. HI, MOM!
Mama Rose was lying at the door of her hut, protecting her babies, when this little one approached with a nuzzie to let her know he was hungry.

JENNY GARCIA ELFRIDA, ARIZONA

3. VIEW FROM THE TOP
I love the fall view—with the white steeples against the oranges, reds and greens—from Mount Battie in Camden Hills State Park near Camden, Maine.

KELLY LEMM SAN DIEGO, CA

1. PASTORAL TABLEAU

My husband, Steve, and our daughter Arielle frolic in the fall leaves at our farm while Finn, the family pup, howls in protest.

RHONDA ANDERSON CALEDONIA, ILLINOIS

2. A FARMER'S TRIBUTE

Hard work and long days keep the rhythm of life turning in the country.

VIVIAN WALIKAINEN VANCOUVER, WASHINGTON

3. AMID THE MOUNTAIN LAUREL

Cucumber Falls, in Ohiopyle State Park in Pennsylvania, is alluring amid the autumn color. After a series of rainstorms, the rushing water stands out in the glen's darkness, in direct contrast to the colorful leaves surrounding it.

BRAD KAVO PITTSBURGH, PA

1. FEATHERED FRIEND

After a day of hiking in South Carolina's Congaree National Park, this gorgeous barred owl flew right in front of my car and perched nearby.

DANIEL RIDDLE SUMTER, SC

2. SCENIC BRIDGE

As a kid, I loved visiting Packsaddle Covered Bridge in fall.

CAROLYN ANDERSON NEW ALEXANDRIA, PA

3. TRANQUIL WATERS

Mountain Fork River in Beavers Bend State Park near Broken Bow, Oklahoma, lights up in the late afternoon. During one visit, I spotted a lone fisherman amid glowing foliage reflected in the glassy water.

CAROLYN FLETCHER MASON CITY, IA

3

Heart & Soul

Apple season brings together members of the Winston family for their annual Apple Butter Day.

STIRRING THE POT

Generations of a Missouri family gather to make
apple butter and cider for a good cause.

MARILYN STOCKER KINGSVILLE, MISSOURI

Needs some more cinnamon! You'll hear that phrase a lot on a certain Saturday in October when the Winston and Guier families and their friends get together to make apple butter.

On Winston Apple Butter Day, five generations of cousins (I'm a second cousin on my mother's side) make this spreadable delight (it's wonderful on biscuits, bread and other baked goods) and cider to raise money for Blackwater Chapel, a Methodist church in Pettis County, Missouri.

Family patriarch Wayne Winston started the fall tradition 40 years ago and passed it on to the next generation. Today the apple butter-making is overseen by Wayne's daughter Helen Cunningham at the farm of another daughter's grandson, Greg Guier.

In the beginning, all apples were peeled by hand. Nowadays, the apple butter starts out with 48 gallons of donated applesauce, which is divided between two 24-gallon copper kettles (one is over 100 years old).

Cousins take turns stirring. Around noon, about 15 pounds of sugar are added to each kettle. The exact amount is decided by the official taste testers—any cousins nearest the kettles at tasting time!

Helen adds cinnamon and Red Hots (*shh*, this candy is the secret ingredient) at different times throughout the process. The Red Hots give just the right buzz of spicy cinnamon. After several more hours of constant stirring, the mixture is finally declared "apple butter" and scooped into

Clockwise from upper left: Picking apples is part of the fun. Andy Pittman stirs the bubbling apple mixture while his cousin Helen Cunningham adds some cinnamon. Apples go into the press for cider.

Above: The Thursday night spin group is always popular..

A TIGHTLY KNIT GROUP

A shared passion enriches a yarn store with much more than sales.

WARREN VAN OVERBEKE SHELBY, MICHIGAN

When Leanne, my wife, first approached me with the idea of opening her own yarn shop, I was skeptical. "Why a yarn shop?" I asked. "We live in the middle of nowhere!" Besides, I thought, who wants to sit around with a bunch of little old ladies?

To understand the conversation better, let's go back to two years prior. At that time, Leanne and I unwittingly entered into the fiber business after a friend of ours, a veterinarian, asked if we could take on two alpacas she was attempting to re-home. Bringing alpacas to a horse ranch was entertaining, but I wasn't sure what to do with them.

That wonderment led to shearing and selling their fleeces, and then purchasing several more alpacas to expand our new business. Although Leanne loved taking care of the animals and selling the fiber, I always sensed she wanted something more out of the fiber business. That's where we return to the conversation about opening a yarn shop.

"Because I want to sell my fiber!" she replied. "The closest yarn shop is more than 45 minutes away, and there's an empty space in town available for rent."

"Yes, but people can purchase yarn and fiber online!" I cried. "Who's going to come to a small-town yarn shop?"

And poof! Before I knew it, Knit & Spin LLC was born.

Until a recent gathering at the shop, I hadn't realized what I completely failed to understand about my wife's dream of opening a local yarn shop. While it's awesome to raise alpacas in order to sell fiber, it's a solitary and impersonal job. And despite the fact that western Michigan has a large group of fiber farmers, it's not what I would call a tightknit community. Sure, there are gatherings, seminars and fiber fairs, but it's not as personal or interactive as sitting down with a group of talented individuals while they create magnificent articles of clothing from the raw fibers they spin, knit, crochet or weave.

Moreover, spinners, knitters, crocheters and weavers come from all walks of life. I have come to realize that our yarn shop is visited by all—regardless of age, color, race, religion, gender, financial status, political affiliation or national origin. They're not all just "little old ladies."

Yarnies, as they like to refer to themselves, seek out these shops

Clockwise from left: Knit & Spin's alpaca herd consists of two breeds, Huacaya (that's Angus on the left) and Suri (that's Finnigan on the right). Weaving instructor Ann uses a hook technique. The shop helps promote indie dyers and local fiber mills.

> **Yarnies, as they like to refer to themselves, seek out these shops as treasure hunters look for lost gold."**

as treasure hunters look for lost gold. Initially, I thought it was for the yarn, as individuals would enter the shop and browse the selection, audibly oohing and aahing all the way.

But as of late I've determined that their presence in our shop is much more about the camaraderie and community these people share than about the yarn.

Over the last year and a half, I have watched as our little yarn shop has grown—not by sales, but by relationships. Many first-timers who enter comment how warm and comfortable the shop is, which is what Leanne intended.

But I believe her ultimate mission was to create a friendly and sociable homelike space where fiber-minded individuals could gather and share with each other— not just to share their common interests of spinning, knitting, crocheting and weaving, but also their hopes, fears, accomplishments and defeats.

Welcoming and supportive to all who enter, Knit & Spin has evolved into a benevolent community of yarnies who really do love and care for one another. Whether it's helping a rookie knitter with his first feeble attempt at a scarf (yep, that was me) or someone confronting cancer, our community of yarnies is always there for one another.

And Leanne and I have been there for our yarnies during the pandemic, too. We kept the shop open three days a week even in the midst of COVID-19, so they could safely get their "fix." Through the weaving together of experiences, joys and friendships, this has become an uplifting and truly tightknit group.

Left: Visitors to the shop learn to create beautiful designs with two yarns. Right: An expert spinner teaches her craft.

A GRANDFATHER'S LEGACY

This 1948 Oliver 70 is still going strong.

EVAN BRYAN HILLSBORO, OREGON

My grandfather Arnold Leppin worked as a welder in Portland's shipyards during World War II. After the war ended, he decided to go back to farming, using his earnings to start his own operation north of Hillsboro, Oregon. To save money, he designed and welded some of his own equipment.

He purchased this Oliver Row Crop 70 new in 1948. Originally it had implements for cultivating soil—which was ideal for growing strawberries or corn. It also had a six-speed transmission and electric lights, which made moving between fields easier. When my grandfather started his cattle operation, he added a loader so he could haul hay and fence posts. Again, to save money, he built the loader himself, completely out of found materials.

The tractor made an appearance in a movie—*Chrome Soldiers*—starring Gary Busey. Some of the filming took place on our farm, and the director worked some of our equipment into the storyline. In the film, the Oliver breaks down right before a crucial harvest. (Obviously I'm glad this was fictional.)

Today, our farm produces wheat, red clover, grass seed and timber. My grandfather passed away in 2006, and I wanted to keep the Oliver running as a tribute to him. I use it to haul hay, lumber and other materials around the farm. It starts after one crank and still has good power. The only updates I've had to make were new battery cables and a rebuilt starter. Oliver definitely made its tractors to last! In fact, this "antique" has towed some of our newer tractors after they've broken down in the field. My plan is to pass the 70 along to the next generation. I'm sure it will serve them well.

I am proud to build on my grandfather's legacy and to farm the same land that he and his father did. This is truly an example of the American dream.

Right: Arnold Leppin hand built the loader for his Oliver 70. Above: Two generations later, the machine is still in use on the family's Oregon farm.

Taste of the Country

SAVOR THE FLAVORS OF THE SEASON

HERB-GLAZED TURKEY

PREP 10 min.
BAKE 3½ hours + standing
MAKES 18 servings

1	turkey (14 to 16 lbs.)
¼	cup olive oil
2	tsp. dried thyme
1½	tsp. salt, divided
1¼	tsp. pepper, divided
1	cup honey
1	cup corn syrup
¼	cup butter, melted
2	tsp. dried rosemary, crushed
1	tsp. rubbed sage
1	tsp. dried basil

1. Brush turkey with the oil; tie the drumsticks together. Place turkey breast side up on a rack in a roasting pan. Combine the thyme, 1 tsp. salt and 1 tsp. pepper; sprinkle evenly over turkey. Bake, uncovered, at 325° for 2 hours.

2. In a small bowl, combine the honey, corn syrup, butter, rosemary, sage, basil, and the remaining ½ tsp. salt and ¼ tsp. pepper. Brush over turkey. Bake until a thermometer inserted in thickest part of thigh reads 170°-175°, about 90 minutes longer, basting frequently with the pan drippings. Cover loosely with foil if turkey browns too quickly.

3. Remove turkey from the oven. Cover turkey and let stand for 15 minutes before carving.

7 OZ. COOKED TURKEY 570 cal., 25g fat (8g sat. fat), 197mg chol., 380mg sod., 30g carb. (24g sugars, 0 fiber), 56g pro.

MAPLE-GLAZED GREEN BEANS

TAKES 25 min. **MAKES** 4 servings

- 3 cups cut fresh green beans
- 1 large onion, chopped
- 4 bacon strips, cut into 1-in. pieces
- ½ cup dried cranberries
- ¼ cup maple syrup
- ¼ tsp. salt
- ¼ tsp. pepper
- 1 Tbsp. bourbon, optional

1. In a large saucepan, place steamer basket over 1 in. of water. Place beans in the basket. Bring water to a boil. Reduce the heat to maintain a low boil; steam, covered, until beans are crisp-tender, 4-5 minutes.

2. Meanwhile, in a large skillet, cook the onion and bacon over medium heat until bacon is crisp; drain. Stir cranberries, syrup, salt, pepper and, if desired, bourbon into onion mixture. Add beans and heat through, tossing to combine.

¾ CUP 173 cal., 3g fat (1g sat. fat), 7mg chol., 302mg sod., 35g carb. (24g sugars, 4g fiber), 4g pro.

MOM'S SWEET POTATO BAKE

PREP 10 min. **BAKE** 45 min.
MAKES 8 servings

- 3 cups cold mashed sweet potatoes (prepared without milk or butter)
- 1 cup sugar
- 3 large eggs
- ½ cup 2% milk
- ¼ cup butter, softened
- 1 tsp. salt
- 1 tsp. vanilla extract

TOPPING

- ½ cup packed brown sugar
- ½ cup chopped pecans
- ¼ cup all-purpose flour
- 2 Tbsp. cold butter

1. In a large bowl, beat sweet potatoes, sugar, eggs, milk, butter, salt and vanilla until smooth. Transfer to a greased 2-qt. baking dish.

2. In a small bowl, combine the brown sugar, pecans and flour; cut in butter until crumbly. Sprinkle over potato mixture. Bake, uncovered, at 325° for 45-50 minutes or until a thermometer reads 160°.

½ CUP 417 cal., 16g fat (7g sat. fat), 94mg chol., 435mg sod., 65g carb. (47g sugars, 4g fiber), 6g pro.

CHORIZO PUMPKIN PASTA

TAKES 30 min. **MAKES** 6 servings

- 3 cups uncooked gemelli or spiral pasta (about 12 oz.)
- 1 pkg. (12 oz.) fully cooked chorizo chicken sausage links or flavor of choice, sliced
- 1 cup canned pumpkin
- 1 cup half-and-half cream
- ¾ tsp. salt
- ¼ tsp. pepper
- 1½ cups shredded Manchego or Monterey Jack cheese
  Minced fresh cilantro, optional

1. Cook pasta according to package directions. Drain, reserving ¾ cup pasta water.
2. Meanwhile, in a large skillet, saute sausage over medium heat until lightly browned; reduce heat to medium-low. Add pumpkin, cream, salt and pepper; cook and stir until heated through. Toss with pasta and enough pasta water to moisten; stir in cheese. If desired, sprinkle with cilantro.

1⅓ CUPS 471 cal., 20g fat (11g sat. fat), 92mg chol., 847mg sod., 48g carb. (7g sugars, 3g fiber), 26g pro.

PUMPKIN SLOPPY JOES

TAKES 30 min. **MAKES** 8 servings

- 1 lb. ground beef
- ½ cup chopped onion
- 1 garlic clove, minced
- 1 cup canned pumpkin
- 1 can (8 oz.) tomato sauce
- 2 Tbsp. brown sugar
- 2 Tbsp. prepared mustard
- 2 tsp. chili powder
- ½ tsp. salt
  American and mozzarella cheese slices
- 8 hamburger buns, split

1. In a large skillet, cook beef, onion and garlic over medium heat until the meat is no longer pink; drain. Stir in pumpkin, tomato sauce, brown sugar, mustard, chili powder and salt. Bring to a boil. Then reduce the heat and simmer, uncovered, 10 minutes.
2. Meanwhile, cut American cheese slices with a pumpkin-shaped cookie cutter. Next cut mozzarella cheese into shapes (triangles, half-circles, etc.) to make pumpkin faces. Spoon meat mixture onto buns and top each with a pumpkin.

1 CUP 250 cal., 8g fat (3g sat. fat), 28mg chol., 607mg sod., 30g carb. (9g sugars, 3g fiber), 15g pro.

ROASTED PUMPKIN SALAD WITH ORANGE DRESSING

PREP 45 min. **BAKE** 40 min.
MAKES 16 servings

- 1 pie pumpkin or medium butternut squash (about 3 lbs.)
- ¼ cup plus 6 Tbsp. olive oil, divided
- ¼ cup plus 2 Tbsp. honey, divided
- ¾ tsp. salt, divided
- ¼ tsp. pepper, divided
- ½ cup orange juice
- ¼ cup balsamic vinegar
- 1 Tbsp. chopped shallot
- 1 garlic clove, minced
- 2 tsp. grated orange zest
- 10 oz. fresh arugula or 1 lb. fresh baby spinach
- 1 cup dried apricots, thinly sliced
- 1 cup dried cranberries
- 1 pkg. (5.3 oz.) fresh goat cheese, crumbled

1. Preheat oven to 350°. Peel and cut pumpkin into 1-in. cubes (reserve seeds). In large bowl, toss with ¼ cup oil, ¼ cup honey, ½ tsp. salt and ⅛ tsp. pepper; place in greased 15x10x1-in. pan; bake 30-35 minutes.

2. Wash seeds; spread on greased baking sheet; bake 8-10 minutes.

3. Place orange juice, vinegar, shallot, garlic, orange zest and remaining 2 Tbsp. honey in small saucepan. Boil 15-20 minutes. Strain into small bowl. Whisk in remaining 6 Tbsp. oil, ¼ tsp. salt and ⅛ tsp. pepper until blended.

4. In large bowl, combine the arugula, apricots, cranberries and roasted pumpkin. Sprinkle with goat cheese and roasted pumpkin seeds. Drizzle with dressing before serving.

1½ CUPS 195 cal., 10g fat (2g sat. fat), 6mg chol., 157mg sod., 27g carb. (20g sugars, 3g fiber), 2g pro. Diabetic Exchanges: 2 fat, 1½ starch, 1 vegetable.

APPLE CRANBERRY UPSIDE-DOWN CAKES

PREP 25 min. **BAKE** 15 min.
MAKES 6 servings

- 2 medium tart apples, peeled and diced
- ⅓ cup packed brown sugar
- 1 tsp. lemon juice
- 2 Tbsp. butter
- ½ cup dried cranberries
- ⅓ cup chopped pecans
- ¾ cup all-purpose flour
- ½ cup yellow cornmeal
- ⅓ cup sugar
- 1½ tsp. baking powder
- ½ tsp. ground cinnamon
- ¼ tsp. salt
- ¾ cup buttermilk
- ¼ cup olive oil
- 1 large egg, room temperature

TOPPING

- ½ cup heavy whipping cream
- 2 Tbsp. sour cream
- 2 Tbsp. confectioners' sugar

1. In a large skillet, cook apples, brown sugar and lemon juice in butter over medium heat until apples are tender. Stir in cranberries and pecans. Divide mixture evenly among 3 greased 6½-in. cast-iron skillets.

2. In a large bowl, combine flour, cornmeal, sugar, baking powder, cinnamon and salt. In a small bowl, whisk buttermilk, oil and egg. Stir into dry ingredients. Pour over apple mixture.

3. Bake at 400° until a toothpick inserted in the center comes out clean, 14-18 minutes. Run a knife around edges of cakes to loosen. Cool for 3 minutes before inverting onto serving plates.

4. In a small bowl, beat the cream until it begins to thicken. Add sour cream and confectioners' sugar; beat until soft peaks form. Serve with warm cakes.

½ CAKE WITH 3 TBSP. TOPPING 525 cal., 27g fat (10g sat. fat), 66mg chol., 332mg sod., 68g carb. (42g sugars, 3g fiber), 6g pro.

CIDER DOUGHNUTS

PREP 25 min. + chilling
COOK 5 min./batch
MAKES about 1½ dozen

- 3 cups all-purpose flour
- ½ cup whole wheat flour
- ⅔ cup packed brown sugar
- 2 tsp. baking powder
- 1 tsp. ground nutmeg
- ¾ tsp. salt
- ½ tsp. baking soda
- ¼ tsp. ground cinnamon
- ¼ tsp. ground allspice
- ¼ tsp. ground cardamom
- 2 large eggs, room temperature
- 1 cup apple cider
- 6 Tbsp. butter, melted
  Oil for deep-fat frying
  Confectioners' sugar, optional

1. In a large bowl, whisk together first 10 ingredients. In another bowl, whisk together eggs, cider and butter. Add to flour mixture; stir just until moistened. Then refrigerate, covered, 1 hour.

2. Divide dough in half. On a lightly floured surface, pat each portion to ½-in. thickness; cut with a 2½-in. doughnut cutter.

3. In an electric skillet or deep fryer, heat oil to 375°. Fry doughnuts 2-3 minutes per side, a few at a time; drain on paper towels. If desired, dust with confectioners' sugar.

1 DOUGHNUT 217 cal., 10g fat (3g sat. fat), 31mg chol., 229mg sod., 28g carb. (9g sugars, 1g fiber), 3g pro.

SKILLET STOUT BROWNIES

PREP 30 min. **BAKE** 25 min. + cooling
MAKES 12 servings

- 8 oz. semisweet chocolate, chopped
- 1 cup butter, cubed
- 1 cup milk stout beer
- 1 large egg, room temperature
- 2 large egg yolks, room temperature
- ¾ cup sugar
- ¼ cup packed brown sugar
- ¾ cup all-purpose flour
- ⅓ cup baking cocoa
- ½ tsp. salt
  Vanilla ice cream, optional

1. Preheat oven to 350°. Place the chocolate in a large bowl. In a 10-in. cast-iron skillet or other ovenproof skillet, combine butter and stout. Bring to a boil; reduce heat. Simmer 10 minutes, stirring constantly. Pour over chocolate; stir with a whisk until smooth. Cool slightly. In another large bowl, beat egg, yolks and sugars until blended. Stir in chocolate mixture. In another bowl, mix flour, baking cocoa and salt; gradually add to chocolate mixture, mixing well.

2. Spread into skillet. Bake until set, 25-30 minutes. Cool completely in skillet on a wire rack. If desired, serve with vanilla ice cream.

1 PIECE 363 cal., 24g fat (14g sat. fat), 87mg chol., 229mg sod., 29g carb. (21g sugars, 1g fiber), 4g pro.

Wisconsin's shoreline is a natural art gallery with intricate ice sculptures formed as waves throw freezing water on trees, rocks and other objects.

PHOTO BY JAMES BREY

Winter

The Good Life

FARMING FIBER IN THE LAST FRONTIER

Raising musk oxen requires a sense of humor and a high tolerance for freezing temps.

JAMIE LUCE PALMER, ALASKA

My name is Jamie Luce, and I'm the herd manager at the Musk Ox Farm, a nonprofit organization in Palmer, Alaska. We promote gentle musk ox husbandry and the production of qiviut (the soft wool undercoat of musk oxen) to benefit northern people and educate the public. I worked with many types of hoof stock in my career—including reindeer, elk, mountain goats and whitetail deer—before landing here.

I am in charge of 81 musk oxen that live on 75 stunning acres of land protected by an Alaska Farmland Trust conservation easement. We're in the Matanuska Valley, which rests between the Talkeetna and Chugach mountains. My overall goal is to maintain a happy, healthy herd through gentle, low-stress handling. We socialize our animals so they'll let us herd them out of our pastures on foot and comb them by hand. We name them, with a theme for each age group, but we don't turn them into pets that imprint on us. Their personalities are entirely musk ox.

Our herd is split up into about 10 groups, which we arrange by age and sex, as well as orders of dominance. Assessing which personalities work best in a group is the key to success. You don't want a bossy musk ox to scare less-dominant animals

Survivors of the ice age, musk oxen are more closely related to goats than to cattle. Both females and males have horns, which are tipped at the farm for ease of movement and to prevent injuries.

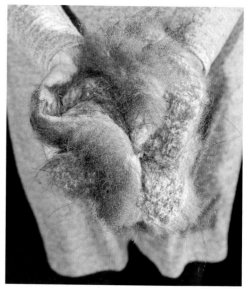

Top left: Qiviut yarn, when pure, is highly sought-after, selling for around $100 an ounce. Top right: Qiviut fiber, seen here just after combing, is smooth, hypoallergenic and eight times warmer than wool.;

into not wanting to come out of the pen. On the other hand, you need a musk ox in charge or you will have a lot of sassy musk oxen, which extends your herding time and keeps you on the run. When all else fails, we bribe them with treats. Since food is their first love, it usually works. They get free access to hay all winter until spring, when the pastures green up.

After a year of calving and combing, rotational grazing and setting up harems, winter offers a welcome reprieve. I spend my days making sure our facilities are maintained, everyone is well fed and the herd has ample access to water or snow.

With temperatures reaching minus 20 degrees this time of year, sometimes in very high winds, keeping the heaters working is critical to prevent their water from freezing solid. This is especially important when there isn't any snow. (Being arctic animals, musk oxen have evolved to eat snow in lieu of drinking water to quench their thirst.) I also track the herd's weight and health weekly and work with the previous year's calves to make sure they feel safe and secure with staff and are ready to be combed in May.

WATER SUPPLIES AND WEIGH-INS

Jan. 15 It has been cold and windy on the farm, and the musk oxen are quite happy. They live for negative temperatures and blowing winds. You will often see them running around, stomping about and doing some super sweet spin moves.

While they were playing, the water pipes in our pastures froze. We need to thaw the pipes before the snow melts or blows away in heavy winds. Otherwise, we'll have to haul water out to the pen in our Greer tank—quite a task in itself.

Normally we weigh our animals on Mondays and Tuesdays. But since I just returned from a trip, we weighed only half of the herd today. The rest will be done tomorrow. It was windy, so the sass was on full throttle. Instead of nicely walking, they ran around the pen—charging and head-butting posts, tetherballs and hay feeders.

I checked the health of all 81 musk oxen as I gave them their daily ration of pellets. I am being a lot more meticulous with health checks this week since I haven't seen these fluffballs in a while.

Jan. 16 During this morning's feeding, I encountered snowdrifts all over the chutes—which made it more difficult to drive through and feed everyone. To top things off, all but one of the pipes were frozen. My maintenance manager, Josh, and I dug out the snowed-in water tank to haul water to each pen.

Two of our older ladies, Medusa and Aquarius, have lost a little more weight than I'd like, so I decided to move them into one of the front pens attached to the barn. Josh and I set up the chutes, and I got a treat bucket ready to entice them.

That strategy may have worked a little too well. Half of the musk oxen in the pen

Jamie loads up the daily pellet rations for feeding.

saw me holding the treat bucket and came running after me as I tried to get to the two I wanted. But Medusa and Aquarius finally had their own hay and water in a pen where they could snuggle up together and get out of the wind.

Jan. 17 I'm facing the fact that our pipes will stay frozen until spring. Hauling water will become the new normal for the next three months. On top of that, one of our water heaters died. There will be a lot of ice chipping and hammering to keep the water flowing until we get it replaced. Josh helped with hay; we skipped doing it yesterday because we didn't want it to blow away during the night. Most of the musk oxen ran alongside the truck until we made it to their hay feeders.

Jan. 18 Saturdays are my quick days; I come in and check the herd to make sure everyone looks good and is in the right place. I also check snow and water. Since all the snow has blown away, I made sure that the water heaters were working and chipped ice out of the tank for the ones without heat. This is never fun, especially when it's freezing out and the wind is blowing. On the bright side, I made it to the feed store to grab a new water heater!

Jan. 20 We weighed most of the herd today. As usual, we had to bribe the misfit group with treats. The main culprits were Little Man, Luna and Safety. Those three were bottle-raised because their moms rejected them as calves, so they imprinted on humans and don't understand that they are musk oxen. I love them, but they can be pretty rotten!

Jan. 21 Daylight is creeping back; we started weighing the herd at 9:30 a.m. instead of the normal 10 a.m. We began with the old men, who walked through the pasture gate one at a time. That never happens with this group, and it was glorious. Even Wild Thyme and Iron Man walked their way out. Those two are usually the most stubborn; they like to run to the very back of the pasture and zigzag past us. We get winded and start sweating in 10-below weather trying to get them to the barn, but they have a blast!

Fenugreek, one of the bulls, trotted right out. He's lower in the pecking order

and likes to get out of the other bulls' way before the herding starts. The rest came out in two groups, as three of them were relaxing up front while the others were back in the pasture eating hay. Last in line, the young girls from the age groups that we call Spices and State Capitals came out quite easily.

HAIR BRUSHING AND HEAD-BUTTING

Jan. 22 The calves are getting so efficient that they can basically run themselves through the barn now.

I rewarded them today with some willow branches stored in the barn since summer. After handing out treats, I cleaned up the barn—which isn't heated since musk oxen are fully insulated by their qiviut. That means that our scale and the surrounding area get covered with mud, snow and fecal matter that freezes to the nearest surface when we weigh them.

It was still pretty warm out at 15 degrees above zero, so I decided to do some light fencing—fixing wires that have been popped by the animals. I began with the pen used by a group that includes multiple ages of females from the Trees, Candies and Gemstones groups. After 10 minutes,

Jade and Maple moseyed over to see what I was doing, which turned into them hitting the fence I was trying to repair. That was the end of that!

Jan. 23 It was quite chilly this morning: minus 7 degrees in town and minus 10 at work. I love seeing the frosty musk oxen in this weather when the sun is coming up, because they glisten in the light. They look as if they've been in a deep freeze for a month—but unlike us mere humans, they absolutely love it! On cold mornings like these, I get to see them playfully tromping through the snow, hitting tetherballs or stacks of tires, or just getting the zoomies.

Jan. 24 I practice-combed the calves this morning while giving them treats. I can pretty much comb them everywhere now except their heads and faces. Once released, they ran back to their pen and did laps, then decided to battle it out— head-butting each other and engaging in pushing contests to determine who is more resilient.

Gouda almost always wins, which is funny because her brother, Muenster, outweighs her by a good 20 pounds. Once he figures that out, there will be an interesting change in dynamics.

Everyone came running this morning when they saw the truck arrive. When they run in the snow, they look like movie stars, with the snow billowing and their long hair flowing in the wind.

Jan. 27 I had to bribe the misfits (mostly the older musk oxen) with treats this morning to get them to the barn for weighing. They are set in their ways and know what they can get away with.

GOODBYE, AQUARIUS

Jan. 29 Today was emotionally draining. I love every one of these animals; they have their own quirks and personalities, and I can't express enough how important they are to me. Unfortunately, Aquarius, one of the ladies I recently moved up to the cozy barn area, was at the point of no return. She has had teeth problems and was down in weight. Combining that with her advanced age of 18 years, we decided euthanizing was the best thing to do.

We gave her a morning filled with pellets, willow branches and fresh hay before she was quietly put to sleep. After she died, we took a liver sample to send into a lab. We do this to make sure our animals aren't deficient in any important trace minerals—Alaska's soil and hay are known for a lack of copper and selenium.

Jan. 30 We move the hay feeders in our pastures at least once a week so they don't freeze to the ground and the leftover hay doesn't build up. That makes it much easier to clean up once spring arrives. This is always a two-person job, because musk oxen like to escape. They also like to stand and walk right in front of us as we move things with the tractor, requiring careful driving even at only 2 mph.

Jan. 31 Most of the musk oxen had a dusting of snow on them this morning. I watered everyone since there wasn't much snow last night and the wind is expected to pick up this weekend. The tank takes 15 to 25 minutes to fill depending on water pressure, so I generally leave it going while I multitask. Apparently, that was a bad idea today. The hose fell off the front of the tank, and water went into the tank and then right back out, covering the ground and creating an ice rink. Happily, I was able to fix it and water the herd.

Feb. 3 Little Man had broken part of a toenail, and I trimmed it up for him. Most

Top: Membership and communications coordinator Kerry Nelson leads a farm tour.
Above: Maintenance manager Josh Williams loads hay, which the musk oxen eat freely all winter.

Musk oxen are coming in hot for their weekly weigh-ins.

of the time we let their nails break off naturally and don't need to intervene. It's a lot harder to cut their nails when it's really cold. Josh kept Little Man occupied with treats while I cut off the broken nail and trimmed one of his longer nails to prevent this from happening again.

Everyone was excited for the new bales of hay, as wind had blown away what was left. All the penned musk oxen chased the truck and stole bites of hay as we went by. (Each one eats about a bale of hay per week during the winter when they don't have pasture grass to eat.) Later I was able to connect with one of my future summer interns to go over the basics and plan potential arrival dates in April.

HORN TRIMS AND HEAT WAVES

Feb. 4 All the animals on our farm get their horns tipped so they don't injure themselves or any of us. They don't have predators to worry about here, and it's easier for them to get through smaller areas when they are not bumping into things or poking each other in the process.

Today's lucky three were Argon, Magpie and Eider. We moved them to the weigh scale and then gave each of them a light sedative—we want them comfortable and relaxed but not fully asleep. The sawing took less than 20 seconds per side, then the sedatives were reversed and they were allowed to fully wake up before we put them in a recovery pen.

Feb. 5 Josh and I dug out the young girls' gate—a corner where all the snow collects when it's windy—so we could weigh them. We pushed the three who

got their horns trimmed yesterday back into their original pasture. Next we ran the calves through the barn and into the stall for their "combing" session. The barn pen does not have a hay feeder, so we normally use a water trough to hold hay—which can get messy. Josh built a mini hay feeder (just big enough to hold one bale) out of an old gate and some spare fencing that was too small to use anywhere else. Now we will be able to keep this pen cleaner with a lot less work.

Feb. 6 We seem to be having a heat wave—today it was a balmy 28 degrees! I wore a pair of leggings, a hoodie and my boots and was still hot. Josh and I kept the windows on the truck rolled down as we supplied hay to all the pens.

Feb. 7 I worked on "Herd Happenings," an article for the newsletter we send to Friends of the Musk Ox—a worldwide community of folks who look for ways to become more involved and support the farm. (Learn more about membership at *muskoxfarm.org/fomo*.) I also had a ton of new musk ox research papers to read courtesy of Dani, our education director.

Feb. 10 Monday weigh day! It went quickly since the warmer weather meant the musk oxen weren't very sassy. I was excited to see that Medusa had gained 15 pounds this week! I also figured out drug doses for tomorrow, when we will trim the horns of the other almost-3-year-olds. Since we lightly sedate them during this process, I need to calculate how much sedative to give each one.

Feb. 11 Our two male groups were all punks today; everyone was spry and no one wanted to come out of their pens. Josh, Mark (the farm's executive director) and I got a workout, zigzagging back and forth in the line/wall we created to keep them from getting past us. After the boys were done, we trimmed horns. Wren, Osprey and Teal all looked lovely with their new "haircuts."

Feb. 12 When the wind blows like it did today, it's too miserable to do much outside. After Josh and I pushed the girls back from their recovery pen into their original pasture, I returned to the office to work on data. I figured out the updated lifespan of a musk ox on our farm (it was 18 years, although the oldest, GeorgeAnn, is now 26) as well as the average amount of

qiviut per adult (4 to 5 pounds a year), among other things.

Feb. 13 We were trying to move hay feeders when I opened a gate and Little Man made his move! Since he's not afraid of us or any type of machinery, he breezed past us and went for a brisk morning jog. It was amazing to see him move so fast when 99.9% of the time he moves like a turtle. Once he heard the grain shaking in the treat bucket, though, he was on his way back. So was the rest of this group, coming straight for the gate we needed him to go through. Little Man and his gang got a second breakfast.

Feb. 14 Wednesday's wind caused drifts in the parking lot and alleyways, making driving difficult. Josh was on the tractor all day snowblowing and making sure we were able to get things done. Then the wind blew all the snow away again. So I filled my water tank, turned on the water heaters and filled up the tanks again.

Postscript: It's still winter, and we continue to take care of the herd: slinging hay, chipping ice, shoveling snow and herding animals into the barn when it's not too icy.

Once spring brings melting snow and longer days, things will start ramping up. We'll need to get ready for calving season, pasture rotation and qiviut combing! I'll hire two interns to help me through the spring and summer months. Our interns are especially helpful during April (babies being born) and May (constant combing), our busiest times of the year.

With more than 80 animals to comb, it's time-consuming work. It's also very satisfying to see the scruffy animals become sleek and to fill bags with harvested qiviut!

Editor's Note: Jamie tells us that her 2020 interns worked at the farm despite the pandemic. One of them, Alycia, was a local—so her experience went smoothly, Jamie says. The other, Mychelle, who flew in from Maryland for the opportunity, needed to quarantine in the intern trailer for two weeks before she could come into contact with any of the other employees. That's dedication!

Situated between the Talkeetna and Chugach mountains, the farm's land is protected by an Alaska Farmland Trust conservation easement, ensuring these animals a happy home for the foreseeable future.

OUR BELOVED CENTURY FARM

Like the generations that came before, this family loves
living on the land.

ASHLEY FORD HAMILTON, MISSOURI

The farm that my husband, Robert, and I call home has been in his family since 1893, when it was purchased by Thomas J. Watson and his wife, Abbie.

Robert is the sixth generation to live in our house in Hamilton, Missouri, the birthplace of J.C. Penney. After doing some research at the county courthouse, I learned that our house was built around 1870. The earliest (and only) picture we have of our house before it caught on fire was taken around 1920. Thankfully, only a portion of the house was damaged in the fire, and the family turned that section into a beautiful porch. When we moved to

the farm, we remodeled the old house to look as it did in the 1920 photograph.

While sitting on one of our porches, I take in the best scenic views around. From deer walking by in the early morning fog to orioles tapping on the windows or bullfrogs and crickets being noisy at night, the sights and sounds are something to be admired. We currently have a set of twin deer that live on the farm. I named them Ava and Ida because I like to name all animals. Every day I see a new creature join the menagerie.

Our dog, Cooper, loves living in the country probably just as much as I do, if not more! He, too, enjoys sitting on the patio and listening to all the noises. A side-by-side ranger, a truck or a wagon is always there for him to ride on. Cooper also enjoys swimming, and he has many ponds to choose from. We leave him at home if we go fishing, because he usually goes straight to the pond and scares the fish away.

Living on a farm is not for everyone. Each day is full of hard work, and sometimes it's difficult to find a free moment. Even though this land is not our primary source of income (Robert's dad and brother grow corn and soybeans here), keeping it in tiptop shape can be a full-time job. Luckily, I was raised by

Clockwise from left: The farm has been in Robert's family for six generations. Ashley and Robert love to play in the outdoors. Unless the couple is fishing, Cooper is sure to be right by their side.

parents who taught me to work hard, and I married into a family that shares those same values.

Family is what helps keep the farm going. Watching our son mow the lawn, knowing he is the seventh generation to have lived here, is really special to me. My husband and I cherish looking out the kitchen window and seeing our nephews fishing in the pond. This year my nieces and I canned some of the produce from our garden. Some of the kids were also helpful with picking peas—it might have been their favorite activity, and we may have eaten more while picking than we put in the bucket to bring in for cooking. Letting them all pick a pumpkin grown on our farm was exciting, too. I'd never planted a garden as large as the one we did this year, and we never planned for pumpkins before. They were huge!

It is intriguing to look out over the farmland and wonder what it was like for my husband's family to live and work here so long ago. Many years of hard work, love, dedication and determination have gone into keeping this farm in the family, but I would be willing to bet not one person complained.

To live on a farm is to feel satisfied after a long day, grateful for so many family members helping out, and relaxed to be outside in nature's wonders.

This place is more than just a century farm full of history. It is our home.

Clockwise from the left: Robert brings home the catch of the day. Ashley and her nieces can goods from the garden. Quilts dry in the sunshine.

> ❝ **Many years of hard work, love and dedication have gone into this farm.**❞

THEY DIDN'T GIVE A HOOT

A country couple's owlish ploy was no match for the wisdom of birds.

JILL MANSOR PILESGROVE, NEW JERSEY

The woman looked alarmed as she examined the contents of my husband's cart at the feed and farm store while they waited in line to check out. "I wouldn't buy that if I were you," she said, indicating the decoy owl in his basket.

He'd picked it up in hopes it would scare away the pesky birds that seemed to prefer wintering in our garage to spending the cold months outside. My husband—a no-nonsense kind of guy—asked her to explain what she meant.

"Well," she said, smiling, "we bought a fake owl to scare the birds away from our garage. We thought we'd found the perfect solution to our problem—until a real owl fell in love with the decoy and wouldn't let us in the garage."

My husband was incredulous.

"I am not kidding," the woman said. "We tried to scare the real owl away, but he was unfazed. The fake owl served its purpose, all right—the birds left our garage—but now we had a new problem in the form of a live owl that assaulted us every time we set foot in our own garage. We had to throw out the fake owl for our tormentor to leave. It was a few weeks before he gave up and flew away for good."

Upon concluding this cautionary tale, the woman repeated, "I would not buy that owl if I were you." She cocked her head, trying to assess whether my husband would heed her advice.

The other shoppers in line were enjoying the story, and a few chimed in with stories of their own about owls they had on their own farms or the nuisance birds that insisted on building nests where they weren't welcome.

At last my husband reached the register. He placed the owl decoy on the counter, weighing the pros and cons of inviting an amorous owl to the garage versus hosting a flock of irksome birds. Deciding that he preferred the prospect of the owl, he fished out his wallet.

"Good luck!" The woman called as he left the store with the owl decoy tucked under his arm.

"I sure hope I don't need it!" he responded with a smile.

As soon as my husband got home, he regaled me with the details of his encounter at the store. I had a hard time believing that a real owl would ever truly fall for a fake, but we had a good chuckle and set the decoy up in our garage.

I wish I could say the owl ploy was a success, but the resident squatters weren't the least bit daunted; they might as well have laughed at the cheap imitation. Nor did a real owl come to make a mate of my husband's purchase, which also might have proved effective.

The sparrows still build their nests on the automatic garage door box, and the blackbirds squawk in loud protest when we shoo them away from our Great Pyrenees' food.

1. BLOOMING SPIRIT

The poinsettia business is changing, but the joy of nurturing Christmas' favorite flower stays true.

MERV WEBB HARRISONBURG, VIRGINIA

2. THE LONG HAUL

My parents, Buster and Pat, worked side by side on their Wayan, Idaho, cattle ranch for 51 years. I grew up on the ranch, where we fed cows with a team and sleigh in the winter. Both of my folks are gone now, but this photo by Adonia Henry captures who they were.

RUTH GOWANS CEDAR VALLEY, UTAH

3. STRANDED TRAVELER

This mountain bluebird, typically found in the higher areas of Colorado, was displaced by a late winter storm that likely brought it down to the lower lands in search of food. This photo was taken during the start of the COVID-19 lockdown, so I could relate to the situation of this bird: disoriented, alone and waiting for the storm to pass.

LAURIE NORMANDEAU LONGMONT, COLORADO

1. IS IT SPRING YET?
An ice storm precipitated seven long days without power, but I think that our Longhorn named Haddie had the worst time of all. She was happy to see spring roll in not long after this was taken.

CANDICE ESTEP LIPAN, TEXAS

2. RUSTIC RETREAT
My twin brother Lloyd's rural "crib" (as we call it) is decorated with family memorabilia including an old sleigh. It's the perfect place to get away and visit with family.

LYNN SENGELE COLLINSVILLE, ILLINOIS

3. A SLIVER OF SKY
We explored Alaska's Byron Glacier last November. Here I'm looking up at the sky through a hole in the ice cave.

MEGAN SMITH ANCHORAGE, AK

3

A BEAUTIFUL MOMENT IN TIME
Muddy Creek in western Wisconsin
meanders through marsh and sedge
meadows that disappear underwater
with spring's snowmelt.

KELLY L. JOHNSON ELK MOUND, WISCONSIN

HOLIDAY ROAD

Christmas lights inspire nostalgia and illuminate the path home.

JOHN SCANLAN HILTON HEAD ISLAND, SOUTH CAROLINA

In the spring of 1968, I was the oldest of seven children living in a crackerbox house in Stoutsville, Ohio, when we moved into what I consider to be my true childhood home, out in rural Ohio on Greist Road.

Our new abode sat on 5 acres, with a pond, a wooded ravine and a meandering stream. There was a front yard where we could play sports and a smaller backyard with a sandbox, swing set and treehouse. We flew an American flag at the southeast corner of the house, next to the driveway, and Dad rigged up a spotlight to shine on it. The place was perfect for raising kids.

I left home at 18 and eventually spent 20 years serving with the Marine Corps. After seven moves within the country and as many overseas deployments, I had seen a lot—but only rarely had I made it back to good ol' Greist Road. Perhaps because of this, I will always remember my last drive home for Christmas, in December of 1982.

The final leg of that journey took place in the darkness of the night. As I drove my Chevrolet Vega along U.S. Route 22, I toyed with the radio dial but found only crackly static. My goal was WLVQ, a station that broadcasts out of Columbus. I knew that when it came in clear, I was almost home.

Turning north at last from Route 22 onto Greist Road, I knew I had just over a mile to go. I craned my neck, turning my head to and fro as I tried to spot our illuminated American flag.

To the left I saw the house where, when I had been a runner in high school, a giant German shepherd always ran and barked as I sped by. Baring his teeth, growling and snarling, the big dog would travel alongside me for the length of the fence, until he couldn't follow me anymore. The Christmas decorations there were humble: a single candle in each window. I still couldn't see our flag.

Motoring on, I passed fields of shocked cornstalks to the left and the right. Then I reached the one-lane bridge and knew I had only a half-mile more to go. As a kid I'd park my bicycle at this bridge and catch crawdads in the creek below.

Cresting the slight hill after the one-lane bridge, I kept looking for Old Glory. When I caught the first glimpse in the distance, my eyes welled with tears.

With just a quarter-mile to go, I slowly passed Dunkle's lane. The fields that Mr. Dunkle farmed were prime real estate for boyhood exploration. I easily recognized the Dunkles' Christmas ornamentation:

a simple string of lights on the barn. All the while, Dad's flag grew larger through my windshield.

Over another small hill I saw the home of a neighbor we always called Grandma Frazier. Our family bought eggs from her and went sledding on her land. Her son, Emmett, painted barns for a living, and one summer, my sole source of income was splattering paint for him. In 1982, Grandma Frazier was in her 90s; her decorations consisted of a miniature tree in the living room window.

With just 100 yards to go, I could see the Christmas lights lining our home and the flag over my driver's side mirror.

I took a turn onto the gravel driveway and heard the snow crunch softly under my car's tires as I passed our basketball half-court and the field where we used to play baseball and football.

Now at last I spotted the Christmas tree framed by the curtains of our living room window. I braked to a halt and saw Dad's American flag flying above. I got a lump in my throat, but then I smiled. I was finally home.

Brothers Joe, Jeff, Jerry and John at the crackerbox house in Stoutsville, Ohio.

Jazzy and Duke (left) pose for a photo, but their son, handsome hunk Hudson (right), couldn't quite fit into the window.

FLOPPY EARS AND HAPPY HEARTS

My love for basset hounds began when I was 10 years old.
Now I have a pack.

MACKY LINEBERRY PIERCE, IDAHO

As my husband and I embark on this new territory of empty nesthood, it seems that all of our basset hounds—a pack that includes Duchess Jasnae "Jazzy," Grand "Duke" and their son Big Hunk "Hudson"—are becoming even more like our kids. I often say that to know a basset hound is to love and be loved.

One wintry day after we had finished up a project at my husband's sawmill, we wanted to see if we could get a Christmas picture with our three dogs in one of the old trucks parked nearby. As it turned out, they couldn't get all three of their heads out the same window at the same time—but not for lack of effort! At least we tried.

Our dogs love to play outside in the snow together. With their tails wagging and their noses to the ground, they plow through the cold blanket of white as they search for new odors. Back inside, they start baying for carrots—their favorite treat—before lounging by the fireplace. All the while, they're hoping for the usual cuddles and belly rubs. Sloppy kisses are offered in return.

My husband picks a new favorite every day, but I love them all, along with their little quirks. However, it is Hudson who worships the ground I walk on—until his olfactory system kicks in and suddenly he doesn't know who I am, yet alone listen to me! But at the end of the day, he's another giant lap dog and all hearts are content.

THE SLOW WAY HOME

A tractor, a trailer, a bicycle and a whole lot of snow
made for one unforgettable journey.

RAYMOND BERGTHOLD DUNCANVILLE, TEXAS

I was born on a farm in western Oklahoma in 1928 and lived in Oklahoma and Arkansas until age 15. By then, the country had entered World War II. Two of my brothers and one sister were in the military, and my parents decided to move to Iowa to help the oldest brother with his dairy farm.

We never got accustomed to the freezing temperatures, nor to the snow and ice, so when my brother Ernest was discharged from the military in 1945, our dad decided it was time to return home. He bought a 100-acre farm south of Gentry, Arkansas. He also bought a 1939 Ford 9N with all the latest implements and a flatbed trailer to haul everything south.

Ernest and I offered to help move. To prepare the tractor for driving in winter, we built a fully enclosed cab with windows and a door, and cut up a tubular bed frame to fit over the exhaust manifold to transfer heat from the four-cylinder engine into the cab. We left in late January, and our parents left three days later in their car.

Departing from our brother's farm with hundreds of miles ahead of us, Ernest and I traveled no more than 20 miles per hour in high gear. The second day delivered clear roads, and the tractor performed flawlessly. We had a bit of excitement when a long steam-powered freight train ran alongside us for a distance. The engineer blew a whistle and waved enthusiastically. He looked surprised by what he saw.

In addition to the farm tools, the trailer held my Ward's Hawthorne bike, which I had used back when I was delivering newspapers. Ernest thought it would be fun to take it for a spin. He tied a short rope to a rear corner of the trailer and, holding on to a knot at the other end, he got a fast ride without even pedaling. This worked fine going uphill, but going down, the rope got tangled between the bicycle's fork and front wheel.

I kept driving, unaware of what was happening, so Ernest had no choice but to untie the rope on the move. I was taken aback, to say the least, when he rolled up beside me shouting, "Stop!"

On the third day, Mom and Dad caught up with us and we ate lunch together. The next day we rose early and saw snow on the ground—and more coming down. With no other traffic to speak of, we turned off our headlights because the snow caused such a glare that we couldn't see the road. When we lost traction on an icy hill and began spinning out, I shoveled some gravel from the roadside to get us going.

By the time we reached the Arkansas state line, the pavement was clear. That evening, we pulled into the driveway of our new home. We had made it. It was the trip of a lifetime!

Despite the weather, Ernest (above) and Raymond made the most of their low-speed voyage.

Taste of the Country

DRY-RUB GRILLED PORK CHOPS

PREP 20 min. **COOK** 15 min.
MAKES 4 servings

- 1 Tbsp. olive oil
- 1 medium onion, chopped
- 2 garlic cloves, minced
- 1 can (15 oz.) cannellini beans, rinsed and drained
- 1 cup artichoke hearts in water, drained and chopped
- ¾ cup pitted Greek olives, chopped
- ¼ cup dry white wine
- ¼ cup chicken broth
- ¼ tsp. salt
- ¼ tsp. smoked paprika
- ¼ tsp. pepper
- 4 bone-in pork loin chops (8 oz. each)
- 2 tsp. Greek seasoning
- 5 oz. fresh baby spinach (about 6 cups)

1. In a large skillet, heat oil over medium-high heat. Add onion; cook and stir until tender, 4-5 minutes. Add garlic; cook 1 minute longer. Stir in beans, artichokes, olives, white wine, broth, salt, paprika and pepper. Bring to a boil; reduce heat. Simmer until liquid is almost evaporated, 12-15 minutes.
2. Sprinkle chops with Greek seasoning. Grill over medium heat until a thermometer reads 145°, 6-8 minutes on each side. Let stand 5 minutes.

3. Stir fresh spinach into bean mixture until spinach is wilted, 2-3 minutes. Serve with pork.

1 SERVING 530 cal., 29g fat (8g sat. fat), 111mg chol., 1345mg sod., 22g carb. (1g sugars, 6g fiber), 42g pro.

OLD-FASHIONED EGGNOG

PREP 40 min. + chilling
MAKES 16 servings (3 qt.)

- 12 **large eggs**
- 1½ **cups sugar**
- ½ **tsp. salt**
- 2 **qt. whole milk, divided**
- 2 **Tbsp. vanilla extract**
- 1 **tsp. ground nutmeg**
- 2 **cups heavy whipping cream**
  Optional: Whipped cream, additional nutmeg and cinnamon sticks

1. In a heavy saucepan, whisk together eggs, sugar and salt. Gradually add 1 qt. milk. Stir over low heat until a thermometer reads 160°, about 25 minutes. Pour into a large bowl; stir in vanilla, nutmeg and the remaining milk. Place bowl in ice-water bath; stir until cool. If mixture separates, process in a blender until smooth. Cover and refrigerate 3 hours.

2. Beat cream in a bowl until soft peaks form; whisk into cooled mixture. Pour into a chilled 5-qt. punch bowl. If desired, serve with dollops of whipped cream, nutmeg and cinnamon sticks.

¾ CUP 308 cal., 18g fat (10g sat. fat), 186mg chol., 188mg sod., 26g carb. (26g sugars, 0 fiber), 9g pro.

BISCUITS & SAUSAGE GRAVY

TAKES 15 min. **MAKES** 2 servings

- ¼ **lb. bulk pork sausage**
- 2 **Tbsp. butter**
- 2 **to 3 Tbsp. all-purpose flour**
- ¼ **tsp. salt**
- ⅛ **tsp. pepper**
- 1¼ **to 1⅓ cups whole milk**
  Warm biscuits

In a small skillet, cook sausage over medium heat, breaking into crumbles, until no longer pink, 3-5 minutes; drain. Add butter; heat until melted. Add flour, salt and pepper; cook and stir until blended. Gradually add milk, stirring constantly. Bring to a boil; cook and stir until thickened, about 2 minutes. Serve with biscuits.

¾ CUP 337 cal., 27g fat (14g sat. fat), 72mg chol., 718mg sod., 14g carb. (8g sugars, 0 fiber), 10g pro.

CRUNCHY CHILI CILANTRO LIME ROASTED SHRIMP

TAKES 30 min. **MAKES** 8 servings

- 2 lbs. uncooked shrimp (26-30 per lb.), peeled and deveined
- 4 garlic cloves, minced
- 1 tsp. paprika
- 1 tsp. ground ancho chili pepper
- 1 tsp. ground cumin
- ½ tsp. salt
- ¼ tsp. pepper
- 1 medium lime
- 1 cup crushed tortilla chips
- ¼ cup chopped fresh cilantro
- ¼ cup olive oil
- 1 cup cherry tomatoes, halved
- 1 medium ripe avocado, peeled and cubed

1. Preheat oven to 425°. Place the first 7 ingredients in a greased 15x10x1-in. pan. Finely grate zest from lime. Cut lime crosswise in half; squeeze juice. Add zest and juice to shrimp mixture and toss to coat.

2. In a small bowl, combine crushed chips, cilantro and oil; sprinkle over shrimp mixture. Bake until shrimp turn pink, 12-15 minutes. Top with tomatoes and avocado. If desired, serve with additional lime wedges and cilantro.

1 SERVING 230 cal., 13g fat (2g sat. fat), 138mg chol., 315mg sod., 10g carb. (1g sugars, 2g fiber), 20g pro. Diabetic exchanges: 3 lean meat, 1½ fat, ½ starch.

IRISH CREME DRINK

TAKES 10 min. **MAKES** 10 servings

- 3½ cups vanilla ice cream, softened
- ¾ cup vodka
- ½ cup eggnog
- ⅓ cup sweetened condensed milk
- 1 Tbsp. chocolate syrup
- 1 tsp. instant coffee granules
- ½ tsp. vanilla extract
- ¼ tsp. almond extract
  Grated chocolate and additional chocolate syrup

1. In a large bowl, combine the first 8 ingredients; beat until smooth. Set aside.

2. Place grated chocolate and additional chocolate syrup in separate shallow bowls. Hold each glass upside down and dip rim in chocolate syrup, then dip in grated chocolate. Pour drink mixture into prepared glasses. Serve immediately. *Note:* This recipe was tested with commercially prepared eggnog. Melted ice cream should not be stored in the refrigerator, so discard any leftover mixture.

½ CUP 218 cal., 8g fat (5g sat. fat), 35mg chol., 70mg sod., 25g carb. (21g sugars, 0 fiber), 4g pro.

MUSHROOM & BACON SPAGHETTI SQUASH BOWL

PREP 15 min. **COOK** 20 min.
MAKES 4 servings

- 1 medium spaghetti squash (about 4 lbs.)
- 12 oz. bacon strips, cut into ¾-in. pieces
- ½ lb. sliced baby portobello mushrooms
- 2 garlic cloves, minced
- ½ tsp. salt
- ¼ tsp. crushed red pepper flakes, optional
- ½ cup dry white wine or chicken broth
- 3 Tbsp. all-purpose flour
- 2½ cups 2% milk
- 2 Tbsp. chopped fresh sage
- ¼ cup shredded Parmesan cheese

1. Cut squash in half lengthwise; discard seeds. Place squash cut side down on a microwave-safe plate. Microwave, uncovered, on high until tender, 15-18 minutes.

2. In a large skillet, cook bacon over medium heat until crisp, stirring occasionally. Remove with a slotted spoon; drain on paper towels. Discard drippings, reserving 2 Tbsp. in pan. Add mushrooms to drippings; stir over medium-high heat until tender, 6-8 minutes. Add garlic, salt and, if desired, red pepper flakes; cook 1 minute longer.

3. Stir in wine. Boil until almost evaporated, 4-5 minutes. Stir in flour; gradually whisk in milk. Boil, stirring constantly; cook until thickened, 2-3 minutes. Remove from heat; stir in sage.

4. When squash is cool enough to handle, use a fork to separate strands. Serve with mushroom sauce and bacon; sprinkle with Parmesan cheese.

1 SERVING 494 cal., 25g fat (10g sat. fat), 53mg chol., 1085mg sod., 47g carb. (9g sugars, 8g fiber), 23g pro.

DECORATED CHRISTMAS CUTOUT COOKIES

PREP 15 min. + chilling
BAKE 10 min./batch + cooling
MAKES 6 dozen (2½-in. cookies)

- ¾ **cup butter, softened**
- 1 **cup sugar**
- 2 **large eggs, room temperature**
- 1 **tsp. vanilla extract**
- 2¾ **cups all-purpose flour**
- 1 **tsp. baking powder**
- ½ **tsp. salt**
  Tinted frostings, colored sugars, edible glitter and nonpareils

1. In a large mixing bowl, cream butter and sugar until light and fluffy, 5-7 minutes. Add the eggs and vanilla; mix well. Combine flour, baking powder and salt; gradually add to the creamed mixture; mix well. Chill until firm, about 1 hour.

2. On a lightly floured surface, roll out dough to ¼-in thickness, then cut out with cookie cutters. Using a floured spatula, transfer the cutout cookies to greased baking sheets. Bake at 375° until lightly browned, 8-10 minutes. Cool completely on wire racks.

3. Decorate cookies as desired with frosting, colored sugars and other decorations.

1 UNFROSTED COOKIE 47 cal., 2g fat (1g sat. fat), 11mg chol., 43mg sod., 6g carb. (3g sugars, 0 fiber), 1g pro.

CREAMY CARAMELS

PREP 10 min. **COOK** 30 min. + cooling
MAKES 2½ lbs. (about 64 pieces)

- 1 tsp. plus 1 cup butter, divided
- 1 cup sugar
- 1 cup dark corn syrup
- 1 can (14 oz.) sweetened condensed milk
- 1 tsp. vanilla extract

1. Line an 8-in. square pan with foil; grease foil with 1 tsp. butter and set aside.

2. In a large heavy saucepan, combine sugar, corn syrup and remaining 1 cup butter; bring to a slow boil over medium heat, stirring constantly. Boil slowly for 4 minutes without stirring.

3. Remove from the heat; stir in condensed milk. Reduce heat to medium-low and cook until a candy thermometer reads 238° (soft-ball stage), stirring constantly. Remove from the heat; stir in vanilla.

4. Pour into prepared pan (do not scrape saucepan). Cool. Using the foil, lift candy out of pan. Discard foil; cut candy into 1-in. squares, using a sharp knife sprayed with cooking spray. Wrap caramels individually in waxed paper; twist ends to secure.

1 PIECE 72 cal., 3g fat (2g sat. fat), 10mg chol., 45mg sod., 10g carb. (8g sugars, 0 fiber), 1g pro.

EGGNOG CHEESECAKE

PREP 15 min. + cooling
BAKE 45 min. + chilling
MAKES 16 servings

- 1 cup graham cracker crumbs
- 2 Tbsp. sugar
- 3 Tbsp. butter, melted

FILLING

- 3 pkg. (8 oz. each) cream cheese, softened
- 1 cup sugar
- 3 Tbsp. all-purpose flour
- 2 large eggs, room temperature, lightly beaten
- ¾ cup eggnog
- ½ tsp. rum extract
  Dash ground nutmeg
  Optional: Whipped cream and additional nutmeg

1. Place a greased 9-in. springform pan on a double thickness of heavy-duty foil (about 18 in. square). Securely wrap foil around outside of pan.

2. For crust, in a small bowl, combine the cracker crumbs, sugar and butter. Press onto the bottom of pan. Place on a baking sheet. Bake at 325° for 10 minutes. Cool on a wire rack.

3. In a large bowl, beat cream cheese, sugar and flour until smooth. Add eggs; beat on low speed until combined. Gradually stir in the eggnog, extract and nutmeg. Pour onto crust.

4. Place the springform pan in a larger baking pan; add 1 in. hot water to larger pan.

5. Bake at 325° for 45-50 minutes or until center is just set and top appears dull. Remove the springform pan from the water bath. Cool on a wire rack for 10 minutes. Loosen sides from pan with a knife; cool 1 hour longer. Refrigerate cheesecake overnight; cover when completely cooled. If desired, top cheesecake with whipped cream, then lightly sprinkle with nutmeg.

1 PIECE 275 cal., 19g fat (11g sat. fat), 79mg chol., 195mg sod., 24g carb. (18g sugars, 0 fiber), 5g pro.

Handcrafted

CREATE A FEELING OF HOME

CHANCE OF SNOW

WHAT YOU'LL NEED
Quilling needle tool
16-in.-long paper strips
Glue
Quilling looper tool
Adhesive
Glitter
Ribbon

DIRECTIONS
1. Using a quilling needle tool, wrap 16-in.-long paper strips to make six 1½-in. circles. Glue ends in place. Pinch 1 side of each circle to make a teardrop.
2. Use the needle tool to wrap another strip into a 1-in. circle. Glue the teardrops around the circle, pointed sides out.
3. Using a quilling looper tool (it looks a bit like a comb), wrap a strip around the top prong and glue it down. Wrap around next prong and up and over top prong. Wrap around third prong and up and over top prong. Repeat to end of strip and glue end.
4. Slide off tool and pinch 1 end. Repeat to make 6 small, tight teardrops. Glue these into place between the larger teardrops, pointed side in.
5. Fold a paper strip in half and roll each end outward into a circle to form a Y shape. Repeat for 6 total Y's. Cut at folds. Glue to outer sides of larger teardrops.
6. Create 6 marquise shapes by rolling 6 scrolls and pinching the outer edges on 2 opposite sides. Glue between the Y scroll loops.
7. Spray piece with adhesive. Sprinkle glitter all over. Repeat on other side. Dry completely. Tie ribbon in a loop to hang.

ANYTHING BUT COOKIE-CUTTER

WHAT YOU'LL NEED
Cookie cutters, various sizes
Scrapbook paper
Ribbon
Scissors or craft knife
Super glue
Hot glue gun

DIRECTIONS

1. Arrange cookie cutters in a circular form, making sure each cookie cutter touches another at some surface.

2. Trace cutters onto back of scrapbook paper. Cut out shapes with scissors or knife. Adhere paper to cookie cutters with super glue.

3. Hot-glue cookie cutters together at their touch points.

4. Hot-glue an empty cookie cutter at the top and loop ribbon through it to hang the wreath.

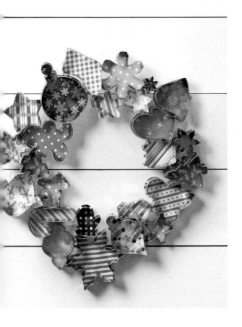

CONVERSATION STARTER

WHAT YOU'LL NEED
Wooden hearts
Craft paints
Cutting machine, letter stickers, or paint pen
Ribbon
Hot glue gun

DIRECTIONS

1. Paint the wooden hearts with hand-mixed craft paints to mimic pastel candy conversation hearts.

2. Use an electronic cutting machine to add names. Or use letter stickers or hand lettering with a paint pen as other options.

3. Hot-glue the finished hearts to a ribbon for hanging.

Craft blogger Hayley Moss of Hull, Iowa, had been dreaming up these wooden conversation hearts for a few years before she finally managed to grab the right supplies from her local craft supply store in time for Valentine's Day crafting. Check out Hayley's instructional video for this project at youtube.com/beefhayleymoss.

> *"No matter how few possessions you own or how little money you have, loving wildlife and nature will make you rich beyond measure."*
>
> — PAUL OXTON

Prairie Smoke wildflowers bloom in Montana's Glacier National Park.

CHUCK HANEY
WHITEFISH, MONTANA